MW00571804

ACKNOWLEDGEMENTS

I've always been a storyteller. I enjoy sharing my life of policing with friends and family. The inspiration for this book comes from my wife, Aleitha to a large degree. When I would tell stories at parties or with friends she would jokingly say, "There's story #12 or story #41." So now I have some of them numbered!

Policing is a rewarding, exciting and demanding life. I don't think I could have gotten through it without the support of my loving wife. She has always been there for me. When I would come home upset about the stupidity or inhumanity of people, she was there to guide me through it, to put it in perspective. The incredibly tough politics of policing would get me down, because I don't and have never played that game. She was there to lift me up.

I don't believe you could go through even one year of policing without having some sort of support system. Seeing assaults on children, women and men, accidental deaths, intentional deaths, suicides, domestic violence, deception, collisions, blood, vomit, broken bones, brains and autopsies, affects you. Without a good support system, it changes you and you become the person you don't want to be.

I also want to thank the people that read the manuscript and helped me with the incredible job of editing. Their thoughts, ideas and suggestions were unbelievably helpful with the flow of the stories. Thank you, Jennifer, Coralie, Aleitha, Laura, Jeff, Trevor, and Walter.

Randy Ward, Retired Cop and Author.

YOU CAN'T MAKE THIS SH#T UP!

Policing Through Stories

Enjoy

YOU CAN'T MAKE THIS SH#T UP!

Policing Through Stories

BY
RANDY WARD

TABLE OF CONTENTS

INTRODUCTION

Being a police officer has been one of the greatest honours of my life and I am proud to share some of my stories.

All the short stories in this book are true events. I have changed the names and settings of the people involved to protect confidentiality. I'm attempting to show you a small portion of the "unusual or different" events that have happened to me, or to members of my team.

What I hope to convey to you is a snapshot of policing, a glimpse into the policing culture, the violence, the sadness, the humour, the moral code and service and, to some degree my personal policing story.

All police throughout the world have similar stories and have mouthed in many languages: "You can't make this shit up!"

Randy Ward
Retired Cop

A BRIDGE OF COURAGE

There are six shifts left before I leave this life, before I retire.

A call about a suicidal male on the High-Level Bridge comes across the radio.

I drop the drunk in my back seat at the shelter and head to the west side to assist some junior members on the suicide call.

The emergency equipment is blaring as I race over the bridge.

"11-80 (my call sign) to Base, are you 100% sure the trains are stopped?"

"10-4, 11-80 the trains are stopped short of the train bridge, CP Rail confirmed it."

"Roger, Base."

I take the gravel road to the bridge, the chatter on the radio continues.

"He's at the middle of the bridge, hanging over the ledge. He's got something in his hands, but we're still a long way off."

My car races along the side of railroad tracks to the west edge of the bridge, as two parked patrol cars come into view.

The rookie cops are out of their cars and about 100 meters onto the bridge.

The radio prattle continues, "We've lost sight of him, Base we no longer have visual contact."

Base responds "11-11, could he have made it to the west side and gotten off the bridge?"

11-80 replies, "No, we're here, he's somewhere in the middle, he never made it to this side."

As I get out of my PC (police car) I'm thinking, *He jumped or he's hiding somewhere in the crevasses of the bridge.*

"11-80 to 11-02, we'll search the bridge and continue east across it. He has to be somewhere on the bridge!"

As we start walking east across the bridge, I can barely see down the bridge because of the fog and rain, but I spot the suicidal male off in the distance getting up on the 4-foot high ledge, 150 meters above the river bottom below.

"Base, he's up on the ledge, we better get some negotiators here and an incident commander."

"11-80 to 11-02, I'll keep going east, get close to him and try to talk to him. At the very least, I'll see if I can find out who he is."

The supervisor, 11-02, responds, "Roger 11-80, keep me informed."

Walking east along the bridge, the two cops with me both say, "I hate heights." I watch them walk gingerly along the open tracks that have a drop to the river valley 150 meters below.

I turn to my two cohorts, "If we go hands on with this guy, he gets tasered. We're not taking any chances."

They respond, "Roger."

We walk for a while. I get ahead of them because heights don't bother me.

Walking to within 10 meters of the suicidal guy, I note he's sitting on the ledge, looking over the edge.

I say, "Hi, I'm Randy. Can you get down from that ledge, so we can chat?"

The man ignores me. As his feet dangle over the edge, he leans forward.

I think, *this guy's going over, right in front of me!*

"Hey, my name is Randy can you just get down from there?"

He continues to ignore me. I've got to do something to get through to this guy.

"Hey, you know I've got six shifts left before I retire, I don't want to leave with the memory of you jumping off this bridge. Please come down!" I plead.

The 20-year-old man turns to me, stares at me for about 30 seconds and says, "My name's Joe."

I've got him talking, that's good, I hope.

I notice that sitting next to Joe on the ledge is a well-used skateboard. He picks it up and hits himself several times hard in the center of his forehead.

I think, *He's attempting to knock himself out and fall. He doesn't have the fortitude, courage or wherewithal to jump.*

"Joe, don't do that! Just chat with me please! I know things are rough with you or you wouldn't be up here, but believe me, I can help! Joe, what's your last name?"

He stops and gives it to me.

I tell my guys, "Run his name."

I continue to try and get through to him, to get him talking. "Joe, can you come down off the ledge, so we can talk? I've got nothing in my hands, I can't hear you very well. I'm just going to come a little closer. Is that ok?"

He responds, "Sure."

Now, I'm about 3 meters from him. He's got a hoodie up, so he can't see me.

All kinds of thoughts go through my head. *Can I rush him, pull him down? What if he falls? He's going to pull me with him! Great; six shifts left, and I get killed on the job; fantastic!*

I decide I'll just keep trying to talk to him.

"Joe, I know things are rough, but I can help. I've been around a long time as you can see from the grey hair."

He turns, stares at me, sizing me up for about a minute and then he climbs down from the ledge.

I think, *ok we have to get close to him, so he doesn't get back up on the ledge.*

"Joe, I'm going to come closer to you, ok?"

"Sure" he says.

Getting on the left side of him, I note his hands are glued to the edge of the rail, like he can just vault himself up whenever he wants.

"Joe, you and I are going to walk off this bridge together, ok?"

He doesn't respond. I keep trying; nothing.

"Joe, we have to get ourselves off this bridge. I'm going to take your left arm; my partner is going to take your right arm."

My partner is a bear. He's a 6'-2" young cop in great shape. He takes hold of Joe's right arm.

"Joe, let go of the edge."

"No," is the response, he tries to climb back up.

"Joe quit resisting," I yell.

I force one of his hands off the rail. He starts fighting with us.

This is not good; we're both going through the tracks to our death if I don't stop this.

My partner grabs him in a bear hug. The guy keeps fighting.

"Cuff him Randy." He says.

I get one cuff partially on; he's fighting to get back up on the ledge.

I can see the river bottom 150 meters below through the gaps in the tracks. It's slippery, we're going to fall through, we have to stop this!

I'm reaching for my Taser when the second rookie cop finally reaches us with his Taser out.

He yells numerous times, "Quit resisting or you're getting tased!" Joe keeps fighting.

Desperately I yell, "Tase him!"

The Taser hits him right in the middle of his back, you can hear the static discharge.

No effect! He keeps fighting!

The rookie squeezes the Taser trigger again. Nothing, he keeps fighting!

Thinking quickly, the officer moves the gun part of the Taser to Joe's leg for a better discharge spread and yells, "Quit resisting!"

The Taser discharge sounds like wrapping paper being squeezed.

Joe yells, "Wow that hurts! Shit, I'll stop!!"

Joe stops fighting. I get the cuffs on, the fight leaves him, and his body relaxes.

"Joe. You're under arrest under the Mental Health Act. We're going to take you to the hospital," I say.

Joe stares at me, "Man, that shit hurt! You got a smoke?"

I'm thinking, *we almost fall to our deaths, and all you can think about is a smoke! You can't make this shit up!*

I admire the courage of my two partners as we cautiously step across the gaps, onto the railroad ties, making our way back to our fellow officers and the waiting ambulance hundreds of meters east of us.

I look proudly at my partners as we walk. They went on the bridge, and did their duty, even though they're afraid of heights.

We continue our long walk, and a quote I heard somewhere comes to mind. Proudly I say, "You guys have courage. Courage is not the absence of fear, it's the overcoming of it, and you my partners, have courage! You overcame your fear, and you did your job and your duty. Thanks for being there."

DON'T ASK

As with most things in policing, it starts with a 911 call.

Answering the call from dispatch, I pull up in front of the hotel. I see an intoxicated male down and bleeding.

He's bleeding from cuts to his wrists.

I do what most police officers would do: I call for an ambulance.

When the ambulance arrives, they wrap up the cuts on his arms and take him to the hospital.

A few hours later, I get the call to pick up the same drunk at the hospital.

When I arrive, I can see he is still intoxicated, and he has two large bandages on his wrists.

I don't want to cause him more injury, so I put him in the back of the van without cuffs. His bandages are so large I can't get the cuffs on anyway.

Driving eastbound on the highway toward the jail, I notice him duck down and start unwrapping his bandages.

I pull the van over to the side of the highway. I jump out and open the back-van door.

The guy has wrapped the bandages around his neck. He isn't breathing; he's turning blue!

I jump into the back of the van, and slice through the bandages with my knife.

He gasps for breath.

Then I hear a clunk! It's the back door of the van shutting!

Are you frigging kidding me? I'm stuck in the back of a police van, on the highway, with a suicidal male!

As I roll the drunk over and handcuff him, he yells, "Thank you!"

All I could think to say was, "Shut the hell up!"

Sitting down on the ledge, inside the van, I think, *I'm never going to live this shit down!*

I get on the radio, "11-01, I need to see you at Highway 3 and 19th Street right away."

He responds, "Roger."

After a few minutes, I hear the future detective pull up, then the crunching of gravel as he walks around the van.

Angrily I bang on the wall, "In here!"

He comes around, opens the back door, and I get out, extremely embarrassed. He looks in the back of the van. Being a future detective, he figures it out.

I look at him and say, "Don't ask," and get in my van and drive to the jail.

It took years for me to get up the courage to tell that story.

I appreciated the friendship and trust of that future detective, as he never said a word about it, to me or to anyone else.

I HAVE TO PEE

We pull up outside the bar on 1st Ave in response to a fight call. As per normal there are three or four police cars for a fight call. We all get out of our PC's and look around.

I notice one guy who's well known to us. The guy looks like he's been in a fight. The witness approaches us, points at the guy and says, "That's him."

The guy takes one look at us and starts running.

All three of us turn, looking at the relatively new recruit standing beside us. This officer is in great shape. He's an ex MMA fighter and can outrun a deer!

The rookie gets the hint and starts to run after the guy. He takes three or four steps, stops, turns to us and says, "I have to pee!"

It takes about two seconds and the rest of us break out laughing. His face turns bright red. Jumping in my PC, I catch up to the bad guy a few blocks away. I approach him laughing and say, "You're under arrest."

He stops and puts his hands in the air.

I can see him wondering, what in the hell am I laughing about, as I handcuff him and put him in the back of the car.

He keeps yelling at me from the back seat, "What are you laughing about?" I break out even more, thinking about that young recruit's face as he turned and said, "I have to pee!"

NOT YOUR TIME

The call comes in about a suicidal male on a front lawn.

"Base, any method of suicide given? Any weapons?"

Base responds, "Unknown 11-11."

I pull up on the quiet residential street and exit my PC.

An Asian man is standing on the front lawn. I immediately look at his hands for any weapons.

No weapons, but he's got something small in his right hand.

I glance to my left as my partner is just pulling up in his PC.

Focusing my attention back on the subject, I notice a small gas can sitting by his feet. He suddenly grabs it and dumps gas all over himself.

I yell to my partner, "Russ, grab your fire extinguisher out of your car."

The smell of the gasoline reaches my nose and I think, *this guy is for real!*

My hands go up to show him there are no weapons in my hands as I walk slowly closer to him.

"Sir, sir, look at me, you don't want to do that!"

I can see the deadpan look in his eyes.

I get on my radio, "Base get the fire department en route. We have a man doused in gasoline on the front lawn of this residence."

"Sir, what's your name?" He doesn't answer me.

He brings up the small item in his hand. It's a lighter.

He starts to flick it.

Holy shit, I think, *this guy's going to flare-up right in front of me.*

But it abruptly starts raining!

I mean not just little drops! It pours! Like someone turned on a waterfall! We're instantly soaked to the bone!

The man keeps trying to flick the lighter, but he's soaked and shiny remnants of gasoline can be seen floating on the puddles of water accumulating at his feet.

I've never experienced such rainfall in such a short time! All three of us are sopping wet.

Yelling to the man who is still trying to get his lighter going I say, "Give it up, someone doesn't want you to die, it's not your time!"

He continues to flick the lighter and small sparks fly harmlessly from it.

"Put down the lighter and get on the ground."

The man has a puzzled look on his face and he drops the lighter and gets on the ground.

I approach him, cuff him and the smell of gasoline assaults my nose again. It's almost overwhelming.

"You're under arrest under the Mental Health Act. There's an ambulance coming to take you to the hospital."

The ambulance arrives a few minutes later. The paramedics rub some chemicals on him to reduce the irritation to his skin, but he still reeks of gas and they won't take him in the ambulance due to their electrical equipment and the chance of sparks.

"Mr. Smelly" is put in the back of my police car and the drive to the hospital begins. My head is hanging out the window all the way like a basset hound in order to breath.

Upon arriving at the hospital, he's put in the psych room and I await the doctor.

The young doctor arrives about a half hour later and I give him the details. He goes in to evaluate the suicidal male.

Twenty minutes later the doctor emerges and says to me, "I've chatted with him and I think he's going to be alright."

A look of utter disbelief crosses my face and I say, "You've got to be kidding!"

The young physician replies arrogantly, "No, I don't think he's going to hurt himself and he should be fine."

Still amazed and shocked I walk slightly into the room and say to the man, "When this Doc lets you go, what are you going to do?"

The man looks at me and yells at the top of his voice, "I'M GOING TO KILL MYSELF!"

Turning to the doctor I say, "Did you not ask that question Doc?"

He looks down sheepishly and says, "Committed for a 30-day psych evaluation" and walks away.

My thoughts are, *just because you're a doctor doesn't necessarily make you smart.*

ONCE WAS LIVING

The dark cloaks, like the cold sea. It is forever, yet it ends at the manmade light.

I stare over the darkness, hear the rumble in the distance. I see them, the searchers. The light floods over them, like a box, like a tear in the dark: it is frozen to the night.

The searchers break the tranquility of the night.

The deer silhouetted against the moonlight on the hill seem to scream, "Get out, why are you here, this is our forest, our home!"

I am out there. Not by my choice, but by the choice of a selfish youth, who, for his desire, ended the life of a child's mother, who was barely out of her teens.

I hold the point, preventing anyone from entering what is now our zone, our perimeter.

You can hear the dim hum of the generator as it floods forth the light.

The light was needed to move what was once living and is now dead, because of the evilness of a youth, his thoughts only of his pleasure.

The high-pitched whine of the yellow tape hits my ears, as the wind tries to tear it down.

The men work, moving what once was living to find the evidence of the How, the When, the Who and if it's there, the Why.

They, in their spacesuits, move, search and record.

I watch. It doesn't look real, but it is.

I see the pain on the face of the victim's mother. I know others guard the killer of her child in the warmth of civilization.

The irony does not escape me.

Today, the deer move through the river bottom. The only thing they know is the smell of us, but that will fade, and be lost in the wind.

The memories of the slain mother, lost because of the wants and desires of a fledgling adult are etched in the recesses of the minds and hearts of the loved ones, and for a while in the hearts and memories of the ones who serve.

THE PARTNER

My heart is heavy. There is a lump in my throat, and tears are just below the surface. Another police officer has died.

I am proud of the officers who have shown up from all over the country. The church capacity of 1200 is overflowing with the uniforms of my brothers and sisters.

The uniforms are blue, black, red and green. The badges tell of the distance my family has traveled to be here.

I look around and I can't help feeling such a sense of pride that they would come for someone they did not know, but I realize that we all know that it is but by the grace of God it is not I who's lying draped with the flag.

The music is inspiring. We sing "How Great Thou Art" and I feel such honour and humility that the Lord has allowed me to be here. I thank Him for that.

Stories about our fallen comrade are told and they lighten the heart for a moment.

We flow from the church, a rainbow of different uniforms, and proceed to line the street. The bagpipes play the song that still brings tears to my eyes as I sit and write this, and I ponder God's amazing grace.

The funeral procession passes me, and the command is given to "Break off." The colours flow in different directions and I again feel the tears and emotions just below my mask of masculinity.

As I walk back to my truck, I walk with a rookie who says, "I just had coffee with him last week and that was the last time I saw him."

My soul and spirit are lifted as I hear the car horn beep, and I see my wife waiting for me at the side of the road. As I get into the car she states, "I felt the need to be here and connect with you."

I fight back my tears of love and I am so happy and proud that she is my partner.

Later at the reception, we eat, and drink and I cannot help my feeling of delight that my wife is here. I see her look at the deceased policeman's wife and I see the hurt and tears of compassion in her eyes for this woman. I know that she knows that there, but by the grace of God, she goes.

PULLING MY LEG

Being a new police officer is exciting, scary, nerve-wracking and extremely interesting, all at the same time. New police officers all go through an 18-month probation period, which means you can get fired for just about any reason, and they don't have to justify it.

It is one of my first days out on patrol, alone in the van hauling drunks, when I get a call about a drunk passed out on the street.

As I arrive, sure enough the guy is passed out. He weighs at least 300 pounds. Help is called for and we load him in the van.

Upon arriving at the jail and opening the back of the van, I see the guy is still passed out. The jail guards recognized him, but this is my first dealing with him.

Asking him to get out of the van is useless because of his state, so I grab onto his leg to pull him out.

I pull on his leg and it comes right off! I'm holding a leg in my hand, freaking out and thinking, *I just ripped this drunk's leg off, I'm going to be sued, charged, and fired.*

What do I do? My dream career in policing is going up in smoke!

The jail guards see the panicked look on my face and start laughing hysterically. They're are practically rolling on the ground! I take a closer look at the leg and realized it is made of wood. I just had to reconnect it.

"Very funny!" I yell to the guards.

They're laughing so hard they are going to have a hard time helping me lodge this drunk in the tank.

Very funny!

SUICIDE BY COP!

It's dayshift again, on a hot summer's day driving around in my police car when suddenly the radio squeals, "Patrols we have an armed robbery at the credit union on Mayor Magrath Drive."

Hitting my siren and lights, I head to the scene and respond on the radio, "11-11 (my call sign) responding."

I dodge in and out of traffic and get on the radio again saying, "Patrols we've had previous robberies where this asshole has fled the city right after the robbery. Let's get some guys on the exits to the city."

The responses are immediate "11-10 heading south, 11-40 north, 13-50 will go east, 13-60 is west on Highway 3."

As I head to the scene, dispatch provides updates, "Patrols, the subject is armed with a knife and has fled in a white van with a partial plate of Bravo, Bravo Charlie."

Abruptly a rookie police officer states, "I've got the vehicle going westbound on Highway 3 in the 1800 block. Should I stop it?"

"No, wait for backup I'm en route," I reply.

Making a U-turn with my lights and siren on, I head northbound on Mayor Magrath and take the exit to go west on Highway 3.

Looking behind me, I see the K9 officer's vehicle is right on my ass.

"Where are you at 13-50?" I ask into the mike.

The response comes back, "Westbound Highway 3 almost to Coalhurst. I'm about 100 meters behind the van. I'm just following it."

"Dispatch advise the RCMP, 13-50, we are en route to you. K9 and I are at Scenic Drive and Highway 3 west," I yell into my mike.

My speedometer is passing over 230 KPH as we rocket west.

We finally catch up to the van at the exit to Highway 3 as it proceeds onto Highway 23 north.

The K9 unit and I turn off our lights and sirens as I come up with a plan.

I'm thinking, *what do we do now? Surly there is no way this guy is going to stop, he just robbed a bank! By this time, the bad guys has got to know what's up!*

We have a parade, three marked police units following the bank robber and an unmarked unit directly behind the suspect vehicle.

A plan formulates in my head and it spills out on the radio.

"Unmarked unit, pass the subject vehicle, go about a kilometre and stop southbound traffic; 13-60 fall back and stop northbound traffic at the last intersection; K9 and I will activate our lights and do a high risk take down."

All the units respond, "Copy" and head to their positions.

"You ready Jim?" I ask the veteran K9 officer.

"Roger," he responds.

We hit the lights and sirens. To my surprise the van pulls over to the right-hand side of the roadway.

We pull up into a takedown position; about 20 meters behind, slightly angled to the white van. I open my driver's door so I have some extra cover if the van driver has a weapon.

Unexpectedly, the van's passenger sliding door slides open. A large man exits the vehicle.

I get on the radio, "Jim he's going to run into the field. Get your dog ready."

It takes me a millisecond to realize the guy isn't running into the field.

He is running straight at me with a large knife in each hand!

Instantly, my gun is in my hand and I'm yelling, "Stop, Stop!" but he has this look on his face.

He is running full out, his eyes wide and determined, his jaw set. The long black military knives are in each hand.

He knows I have no choice but to shoot him. Suicide by cop!

I'm yelling at the top of my lungs, "Stop!" but I can't hear anything; auditory exclusion has set in.

Nothing else exists except this man running at me, trying to kill me.

My gun is pointed at his chest; he's getting closer; 30 feet, 20 feet, my finger tightens on the trigger. A little more pressure on the trigger until the firing pin hits the primer and the bullet flies, breaking the sound barrier and the lead punctures his chest.

Out of the corner of my eye I see movement. It's the K9 officer's dog running at the guy, my finger slackens slightly on the trigger; the dog jumps at the robber's arm and misses.

The suicidal man stops for a second and looks at me. You can see it in his face: he's lost the will to die.

I yell at the top of my voice, "Freeze!" He hesitates and drops the knives.

"Get down on the ground!" I yell.

The sounds of the world flood back in. I hear the dog barking and the K9 officer yelling, "Get down on the ground!"

The robber drops to the ground and I take a much-needed breath.

Then, the driver's door opens on the van, and a woman comes out running at us, yelling!

My aim switches to her as I don't know if she has a weapon.

"Stop, get down on the ground!" I yell at the top of my voice.

She stops, looks at the guns pointed at her and complies.

I later learn that the woman is the robber's wife and that they made the idiotic decision to rob banks together.

How do you do that? I can't get my wife to cut the lawn with me, let alone rob banks with me!

TEN SECONDS

It's Tuesday. Thank God, it's the last dayshift for a while. I'm sitting in the office doing paperwork with my summer student.

The radio squeals, "Patrols, we need someone to respond to a domestic dispute on the west side." There is a break, a silence because everyone's busy.

I'm thinking, *I've got a ton of paperwork to do.* Suddenly, more details start flowing from the dispatcher. "The male subject has a machete and is threatening a female."

The radio comes alive. "I'll respond."

Another policeman says, "I'm on the west side, I'll head over."

I say, "I'm leaving the station." I throw my paperwork in the corner and we run out back. Shit!! My van's downstairs getting cleaned by the maintenance guy!

We run downstairs and the adrenalin is building inside me. "Come on, come on, move it!" I yell to my student. The damn garage door isn't opening fast enough.

There, it's open; I step on it, and throw on the lights and siren.

Dispatch comes on: "The man's now in the lobby of the apartment building with the machete, he's smashing a vending machine and threatening civilians."

Flooring it! Accelerating down the hill, I hear over the radio, "I'm out."

This frigging pig of a van is not moving fast enough, "Get the hell out of the way!!" I yell at vehicles on the road, but they can't hear me because the windows are up.

The cop who arrived at the scene comes across the radio: "Get me some backup here, I need backup!!"

Responding, "I'm almost there; I'm at the top of the hill."

I hate this frigging van, it can't corner fast enough! I'm up on two wheels rounding the corner, it flops back down on four wheels as it exits the corner. My foot rams the pedal to the floor: the engine roars as the K9 car books out at the scene over the radio.

"Get your dog in here," the first cop says over the radio. Hearing the strain and urgency in his voice, all I can think is, *Get there! He needs help!*

I come screeching into the parking lot. The people in the lot are yelling something at me; I slam it into park.

Yelling at my student, I say, "Stay in the van!"

I'm running towards the lobby; a woman comes toward me. "He needs help, he's got a knife," she cries.

Drawing my gun, I can hear yelling; I can't make out what they're saying. My heart is pounding. Thirty feet from the lobby, there's a civilian holding the lobby door. More yelling! I'm almost at the door!!

Bang! Bang! Pause. Three more shots.

I'm not sure what's happening, it seems unreal. *Is someone shooting at me?*

"Get down! Get down!!" I yell at the guy holding the door.

I come around the corner, broken glass on the floor, my fellow officer standing there, gun out, smoke still coming from the tip of the barrel, like the tip of a cigarette.

Silence. "Auditory exclusion" has set in.

Looking to my right, I see the K9 officer and his dog are there; on the ground is a large machete, still sliding toward us. I'm thinking: *Too close! You let him get too close!*

A man is down; he's on his knees, he falls face down to the floor, dark red blood gushes from under him. I pause for a split second and realize that, for some reason there are no exit wounds.

The man's naked from the waist down, and the rasping of his breath is deep and disturbing. It rattles, like the sound an old man would make when he's sleeping. Then nothing! Silence!

It's so quiet. The mike is suddenly in my left hand.

"Shots fired, get me an ambulance here."

Crossing over in front of the officer who fired, I see the K9 officer and his dog. The sounds of the scene return, flooding all around me. I hear the screaming, the dog barking, the crying.

There is shattered glass on the floor, there is faeces on the carpet where the man had been moments before.

Moving toward the screaming, my gun is leading my body. Around the corner there's a small woman, wearing only pants and a bra.

I say, "Are you alright? Are you hurt? Is anyone else hurt? Did you see what happened?"

Other people emerge out of nooks, crannies and doorways, yelling and screaming. All are walking toward me.

The woman in the bra says, "My husband, he went crazy this morning, he started chopping up the place, chasing people, yelling the Queen wanted him to kill someone; he was going to chop that cop's head off," pointing to the cop who fired the shots.

"Are we going to get arrested? Are we going to get evicted?" she asks.

Another man in a long trench coat approaches. I note the look of absolute terror on his face, in his eyes. He says, "He was going to chop my head off; I hid in the bathroom, is that alright?"

"Yes," I say.

"Is there anyone else hurt?"

"No," he responds.

I grab onto someone in the group of traumatized people and yell, "Is there another exit?"

They don't seem to understand. They're in shock! "Follow me!" I command.

Heading down a hallway I try a door, it's locked; there's another door that says "alarmed." I don't care, I need to get them out of there and I don't want them walking across a body.

I push open the door, and a high pitch alarm sounds loudly, hurting my ears. Time seems to be moving so slowly, just inching along as we exit the building.

I think, *what's keeping that ambulance?"*

Moving around to the front of the building, I start separating the witnesses and yell at the other cops arriving, "Take this witness," and I push him forward; pulling a female witness forward, I say to another officer, "Take her," and the witnesses are doled out to my crew as they arrive.

The wife stays with me. "Is anyone else hurt?"

"No," she replies as I put her in my van.

More cops arrive, the yellow tape starts coming out. My sergeant arrives; he gets the quick details of the event. I advise my superior, who is junior in age, seniority and experience to me, "We need to keep these witnesses separate to get a pure version of the events; have dispatch call for Victim Services and for some detectives."

The ambulance finally arrives. It took forever, but in reality, it was only about 3 minutes. It seemed like an eternity!

I head back to my van to interview the suspect's wife; she keeps saying, "He's going to be alright, are we going to get evicted? Are we going to get arrested?"

She's in shock. I call for a second ambulance.

I exit my van as the rest of my crew is arriving. "Separate the witnesses, get statements, and keep them behind the tape."

The media is there. How the hell did they get here so fast? Flashes and lights are in my face. "Get behind the tape," I tell them.

Radioing for more help, dispatch advises, "Help's on the way."

The second ambulance has arrived, and the paramedics are examining the wife. I pray she does not have to go; I need her statement while it's fresh. She's frail, white, shaking, but she's warming up. She is wrapped in the wool blanket I had given her. She wants a smoke, she doesn't want to go to the hospital right now. The paramedics say she's fine.

The troops start to arrive; the detectives are all over the place. I advise them what happened, and they start interviewing the witnesses. Relief floods over me, I can hand it over to them. It's no longer my scene!

My part now is to get the statement from the wife. I walk back to the van. She's sitting there smoking a cigarette.

With the statement paper in my hand, I say, "Tell me everything that happened since you got up this morning."

As she tells me about the events, my hand is shaking from the adrenalin as I put her story to paper.

I can't help thinking, *if it had been 10 seconds earlier, if I hadn't gotten my van cleaned, it may have been me that shot him. I would have that look on my face, and the smoke would have been coming out of the tip of my gun.*

I'm so angry that it had to be this cop who shot him; he's been through so much, but at the same time I feel relief that it wasn't me.

Ten seconds was the difference! Survivor's guilt, I think.

THE GAME

"I'm sorry for your loss. I don't know what it's like to lose a son. I can't relate, but my heart hurts for you. Are you sure you want to go into the room instead of using the video?"

Our tears flow with those of the father's as he takes his wife's hand. He stops at the door. He doesn't want to see his baby lying on the slab. The pain, the sorrow is too much for him. The mother nods her head. I lead her into the morgue, holding her hand, the tears flow from both of us. Her 14- year- old son lies on the cold metal slab covered by a white sheet.

I lead them out of the morgue and into the lift. I'm not sure they will ever ride in an elevator again without thinking of their son.

I'm standing outside the basement hospital morgue, the morgue technician a few feet away and the couple's son lying under the sheet behind me.

A few short hours ago, their boy got into an elevator with his friends at the hotel and they pressed the button for the top floor, playing the game!

They watched the light for the floors change 2, 3. When it got to 5 they waited a second, and then hit the emergency stop. The car jolts to a stop and two of the boys grab the doors like they have been doing all night in the hotel and forced them open. Hotel security has been trying to catch them all night: it'd been quite a game for the boys.

The elevator car doors slide back, and they see the bottom of the elevator is about 3 feet from the top of the 5th floor elevator doors. Quickly the oldest boy, who knows how to get the floor doors open, reach's across to the latch, push's it up and put his hands between the floor doors and push's them open. He looks down and sees the 5th floor carpet; he bends down further and looks in the hallway.

"The coast is clear!" he yells to his friends.

He sticks his head out and sees the opening to the elevator shaft is bigger than it has been; this is the first time the elevator has stopped that close to the top of the opening. It is dark in the shaft and the darkness stretched to the basement five floors below.

They have to get moving before security comes!

If security catches them, the game will be over, and their parents will kill them!

"We've got to go!" He drops to his stomach on the elevator floor and shimmies to the opening, his legs dangle close to the shaft, piercing the darkness.

His hands are on the floor of the elevator as he pushes! He lands on the 5th floor carpet, seven feet below and yells "Come on!"

The younger brother copies his brother: he gets on his stomach, shimmies to the edge and let's his feet dangle over the edge. He'd would show them again, how much courage he has!

He pushes off, lands on the carpet, falls backwards on his butt and back. He lays for a second on the carpet, surrounded by his triumph.

The duo has been doing this all night, so they invited their friend to come along. This is his first time in "The Game".

"Security is coming, come on Mike!" they yell.

Mike looks out, sees them on the floor below and summon up all the courage he can muster.

Mike drops to the elevator floor but didn't get on his stomach. He sits on his bum and dangles his feet over the edge of the elevator. He can see the carpeted floor only seven feet below.

He pushes off into the opening.

He lands face first on the carpeted floor, but his bottom half, is in the shaft opening. Panic sets in!

He tries to grab onto something, there is nothing to grab onto. He slides slowly into the darkness desperately trying to grab onto the carpet, the opening, anything!

He screams as he descends into the void, the darkness!

The brothers' eyes widen, both boys yell, "Mike," they run to the opening and see Mike as he descends into the darkness. They hear the sounds as he hits the bottom of the shaft.

Tears explode from their eyes and fall down their young faces.

The guard comes up from the stairwell breathing hard. He's going to catch those little assholes. He'd see them charged!

He comes into the corridor. There they are! He grabs both boys by the scruff of the neck! "I've got you, you little bastards," he says.

He looks at them, something has happened. He looks at the shaft and thinks, *No!*

Letting go of the boys he turns his flashlight on and peers hesitantly into the darkness of the shaft. The boy's body is lying below, pierced by the rebar at the bottom of the shaft. He pushes the boys back, further away from the dark opening.

He reaches for the phone on his belt and dials 911.

This leads to me, a few hours later, tears flowing from my eyes and my heart, aching for the couple who lost their son, mingled with thoughts of my son's home, asleep, safe in their beds. A prayer for my sons spills forth from my lips as I enter the morgue to do my job, my duty.

THE SATANIST

My sister-in-law is a great singer. When she was younger, she sang in a Christian group. My wife and I went to her concert. We bought a cassette tape of her and the other singers singing Christian music. For some reason, we ended up with two of the same music tapes.

A few days after the concert, I'm at home waiting to go on afternoon shift, listening to the Christian music. While listening, a thought flashes through my mind, *give this tape to the Satanist youth I'd dealt with a few days before.* Some would say this was a message from God.

I literally stop in my tracks, look up and said "What?" I keep singing to the music, but the thought won't go away.

You see, I'd run into this young Satanist about two weeks earlier when I arrested him for shoplifting. He didn't have a record, hadn't been in trouble, so I chatted with him. He told me he dabbled in Satanism, to which I advised him you couldn't just dabble in Satanism.

I tell him about Jesus, "Now you have a choice, you can't say you don't know about God, now you have to choose, to follow Satanism or change your path".

I don't usually have an opportunity to share my faith, but in this case, it was appropriate.

So now I'm listening to the tape. I look up in the air, for me, I am chatting with God. "Tell you what, if I run into the kid tonight, I'll give him the tape," I say.

I think, *what are the chances of me running into that 18-year-old Satanist on my afternoon shift?* So, I grab the extra tape, go to work, put the tape in my locker and go about my shift.

I start at 5 p.m. and it's a busy night.

I work until 3 a.m. and never think about the tape again. As I drive into the station parking lot at the end of my shift, who comes walking through the parking lot, where he isn't supposed to be? The young Satanist.

The guy's 18 years old, dressed in a long dark leather coat, with dark goth makeup on, and long shoulder-length dark hair. My mind goes immediately to the tape, and I start laughing. *You have some sense of humour God.*

Getting out of my police car I stop the kid. "What are you doing back here?" I ask.

He replies, "I'm just cutting through to go downtown".

"You're trespassing. You're not supposed to be back here, but I have something for you".

I'm smiling; he must think I'm crazy.

I ask him to wait for me, and I go downstairs to my locker, laughing at God's sense of humour and me making a deal with Him. I get the tape, come out and give him the tape.

"Why are you giving this to me?" he asks.

"I'm supposed to give it to you. I don't know why, I don't care what you do with it, but I know I'm supposed to give it to you."

The kid gets a perplexed look on his face and walks away carrying the tape.

Often in the downtown area, I would run into him again.

If I'm walking on the sidewalk, he avoids me at all costs and crosses the street.

I think he's afraid of me, that my words and deeds have challenged him.

I don't know if he ever listened to the tape, but I know I did what I was supposed to do. What God wanted me to do. That's all you can do.

YOU'RE WITH CHRIST

I am many things: a Christian, a husband, a father, a son, and a police officer.

My partner and I get a call to go to a boarding house in the downtown area because of a disturbance.

Upon arriving, we walk up the stairs and we can hear yelling coming from a room on the second floor. The yelling is in this guttural voice. I don't recognize the language. I knock on the door and advise it's the police, but the yelling continues. My partner opens the door. We enter into the small apartment. Sitting on the bed is a male about 40 years old, dressed in dirty clothing. He has a far away look in his eyes. The man is foaming at the mouth, drooling and spitting.

My partner looks at him and says, "Police." He ignores us.

I walk into his vision and say, "Police." He looks up at me, fear comes across his face, and in this low throaty voice he says, "You're with Christ."

My partner is taken back and says, "Shit," as his jaw drops.

I don't know what else to say but, "Yes I am. Now be quiet and answer my questions." He growls in a low voice and backs up on the bed. My partner keeps saying, "Shit," and backs away.

I have seen many mentally disturbed persons in my career, but this guy is definitely out to lunch.

My partner tries to ask him questions, but he just swears and growls in this deep rasping voice. I tell him to answer my questions.

You can see he is struggling. He appears to have no choice but to answer me. His answers are blurted out, like they are forced out of him.

I tell him he is under arrest under the Mental Health Act plus he has some warrants. I reach out to him, but he jumps back in fear yelling, "Not you!"

If I try to grab onto him, there is going to be a fight, so I try another option, I say, "My partner is going to put handcuffs on you and we are going to the hospital."

My partner grabs onto his arms and puts cuffs on him.

He just keeps staring at me, spitting out words, "You're with Christ," and backs away from me.

He is taken to the hospital and committed to the psych ward.

I don't know if he was possessed or just mentally disturbed, but it sure scared the crap out of my partner and me.

THE VOICE

It's almost 3 a.m. I'll be friggin' glad when this afternoon shift is over. I'd better go get some gas, so the dayshift guy isn't pissed at me.

I head north on 13 Street by the York Hotel. I see a guy get out of his car carrying something and walk into the alley.

Why the hell is this guy walking into an alley at 3 o'clock in the morning? Who care's, he's probably just getting something in the alley. I'm tired, I need to get gas, is what's going through my brain as I continue to drive north.

Now I don't know whether it's the voice of God or just police instinct, but I suddenly think, *No, check it out.* An argument develops in my head: *I'm tired, I need gas. No, check it out.*

I know if I don't listen I will regret it. I've learned to listen to that voice, despite the fact I argue with it at times.

I head north to the end of the block, turn my lights off, and drive quietly southbound into the alley. You can hear a slight crunch of the gravel in the alley, and I strain to see as far as possible into the darkness.

Shape and movement appear about 20 yards ahead of me and I turn my lights on.

Standing over an unconscious native male is a young white male. He has a fire extinguisher in his hand, and he's hitting the native male with it.

Hitting my overheads, I yell into the radio, "10-58 in progress, 13th Street, 200 block, east side." The male drops the fire extinguisher and runs south into the darkness of the alley.

Starting a foot chase, I pass the male victim on the ground, where blood is gushing from an open wound on his head.

I desperately want to catch that asshole, but this guy needs treatment or he's going to bleed out.

"Base, I've got an unconscious native male, about 60 years old, breathing, bleeding from an open head wound. Get me an ambulance."

"Other units responding to this 10-58, the suspect is a white male about 20 years old wearing a black hoodie, last seen running south in the alley behind the York."

I start rendering first aid after grabbing the kit and blankets from my PC.

About two minutes later the paramedics arrive and start helping the unconscious male.

A few minutes later, the paramedic comes up to me and says, "Thank God you found this guy, or he'd be dead by morning from hypothermia."

The other police units responding have set up a cordon, but the suspect has slipped through it. Walking to the end of the alley, the vehicle the perp got out of is still parked by the York. Checking the plate, it comes back to a 20-year-old that resides on the north side of the city.

I park my PC in a dark spot near the alley and watch the vehicle. Experience tells me he will come back for it. Sure enough, in about an hour the asshole slips out of the darkness and tries to get into his car. He's promptly arrested by me and two other units.

I charge the 20-year-old with aggravated assault and interrogate him at the station. Apparently, he and several other males had a club going where they went around assaulting homeless people that were passed out or couldn't defend themselves. I have no idea why!

I've just saved a man who would have been dead by morning and solved 13 other assault cases from around the city that night, all because I listened to the voice in my head.

Instinct or God? Some would say instinct, but I lean in the other direction because I've heard that voice before.

THE LITTLE WOODEN CROSS

The little wooden cross has roses added to the sides. It brings back memories every time I go by. My mind wonders, *what memories or thoughts does it bring to other people?*

My thoughts return to that night and my actions.

I skid to a halt, jump out. My eyes examine the scene, I think, *Ok the firemen are working on him, I need to get this traffic under control before there is another collision.*

I radio, "Base, I need two more cars for traffic control."

"Units coming to this collision, stop them from going under the bridge, detour them at 6th Ave. and 5th St."

I stop the traffic that is trying to go around the scene. I yell, "You stay" and point at the two lead drivers. They block the roadway causing the traffic to back up.

Approaching the firemen, I can see the blood smeared on the pillar, like some grotesque artwork. The young teen is jammed between the pillar and the guardrail; the firemen are working on him trying to stop the blood that is flowing from under his helmet.

The motorcycle is two hundred meters down the road. *Man, was he moving,* I think. There's another youth near the firemen, but they are ignoring him because they have their hands full. He's wandering around with his dented-up helmet in his hands.

"Come here, sit down, are you alright? The ambulance guys will get to you as soon as they can," I say. Checking the youth over, I see he's dazed, bleeding slightly from a head wound.

He says, "I was on the back, we pulled away from the light and he gunned it. I knew we were going to lose it, we hit the curb and flew, his head went right into it and I ran into him!

Looking around, I see the young motorbike driver is being loaded up into the ambulance. I yell to the firemen, "There's another one here."

There are cans of beer near where they landed. The cans are rolling on the roadway, like they are trying to escape the scene.

The firemen approach, there's a strange look on one of their faces. Tears are forming in his eyes. He grabs onto the youth saying, "Are you alright? Are you hurt?"

Looking at the name on the back of the fireman's jacket, I see it's the same as the young lad has given me.

I realize what is my worst nightmare: coming across my son involved in an injury accident. The firemen are shaken. It's one of their own.

Grabbing onto both of them, I say, "Come to my van and warm up. Did you call for another ambulance?" "No," he says, so I radio for one.

The father and son hold each other in the warmth of my van.

The ambulance seems to take forever.

"Load him in your truck and take off," I say. The father grabs onto his son, loads him in the rescue truck, and speeds off for the hospital.

Thank God that it's not my son, thank God that it wasn't his son in the back of the ambulance close to death, I think.

The fire captain approaches me. He's shaken, he knows it was his lieutenant's son that was the passenger. "The driver is not going to make it," he says.

Traffic is being detoured, Identification section is on the way, and my work is almost complete.

"Do we have an ID on the driver?"

"No, but his pants are on the ground near the pillar," replies the captain.

Grabbing the wallet from the torn and stained pants, I realize the name is familiar, I know it, but I don't want to remember it. I push the name down inside; force the memories not to come.

Later, alone in my van, the memories come. It's the same kid that came to my place years earlier, and played with my son. It's the same kid I taught in Scouts; it's the same kid with the mischievous grin and contagious smile.

The emotions tumble and turn inside me. I feel such sadness for his father and his mother, whom I know.

What do other people see when they look at the little wooden cross with the cut-out roses on the side? I know what I see.

LESSON LEARNED

In policing you do certain things that are not in a book because you've learned from others' mistakes and your own. Experience is the great teacher.

For example, if I'm going to drive someone home, I always take them to the house, get out of my car, and make sure they're welcome at that house. This was learned from past experiences of dropping someone at the house, where he wasn't wanted.

On this particular night shift, one of the new guys was transporting an intoxicated male home rather than hauling him to jail. I'm not sure why he was driving him home, but I know he was taught to make sure to get out of the car and escort the drunk to the door.

The rookie drove the intoxicated subject to the residential address supplied by the subject, and the intoxicated subject asked the cop not to go up to the front door because he lived with his parents, and he would get into trouble. I guess the cop felt sorry for him, and let him out at the curb in front of the address he gave.

The drunk wandered into the house, got something to eat out of the fridge, and took his clothes off to go to bed. When he wandered into the bedroom, he saw his girlfriend under the covers with only the top of her head poking out.

He went around to her side of the bed, and started hitting the top of her head with his penis! The woman woke up and screamed because she didn't know the guy. In fact, she was an 82-year-old lady who lived by herself.

The drunk had wandered into the wrong house! He quickly grabbed his clothes and ran out.

We got the 911 call from the elderly lady, with a description of the subject. A few minutes later, he was arrested down the street still trying to find his house, still in a drunken stupor.

The young officer came up to me later, and said, "I know now why you escort them to the door."

Lesson learned.

DON'T FALL OUT

It's the start of dayshift and I start it like every other day: I search my PC (police car).

The backseat of the PC is made of a hard plastic for easy cleaning. You would be amazed at what gets on these seats, mostly body fluids like puke, blood, urine, faeces and even semen. So, when I search my backseat, on comes the latex gloves or my hatch gloves.

On this particular day I was wearing my hatch gloves. When I looked on the floor I spied two folded pieces of newspaper half hidden.

Now, if you're a cop you know what's in there.

I think, *Shit Gary, you didn't search your car after you transported your last prisoner.*

Procedure is that, after you transport someone, you search your backseat each and every time. This ensures that if you find something, it's from the guy you just transported. Now Gary, the night shift guy that was using my PC, is known to not quite follow procedure, shall we say. Back to the search.

I pick up the folded pieces of newspaper thinking, *Shit, I don't want to get Gary in trouble for not searching his car, but if this is what I think it is, I have to do something.*

I carefully unfold the piece of newspaper, and sure enough a white powder: Cocaine.

I'm standing with two grams of cocaine in my hand trying to figure out, how I can best exhibit this stuff without getting Gary a reprimand. I must have a word with him about following procedure.

While trying to figure out this conundrum, a 10-300 call comes in.

10-300 is "Officer needs emergency assistance." I can hear the panicked voice of the female officer in a fight with two subjects in the park downtown.

She needs help now!

The cocaine goes into my top shirt pocket and I go to assist the officer.

On my arrival, I see the officer is down on the ground, fighting feverishly with two males. I run over, and tackle one of them and the fight is on.

I get on top of this moron and I'm in an all-out fight with him and my main thought is, *please don't let this cocaine fall out of my pocket.*

The fight ends with us winning, because we can't afford to lose. If a cop loses a fight, he generally loses his or her life, so there's incentive.

Back to the cocaine.

After I book this guy for assault on a Police Officer, I still need to solve the cocaine problem.

I decide, *I'm going to just chat with the drug guys.* It ends up that was the best decision.

The drug unit needed cocaine samples for training purposes with the dog unit, so the drugs got exhibited, while I had a chat with Gary about putting other officers in an awkward position.

But I'm glad the cocaine didn't fall out in the fight: that would have been extremely hard to explain.

I WASN'T DRIVING

You have to like it when luck is with you.

It's 3 a.m. and I'm driving my PC north on 13th Street facing a green light at 5th Avenue North. A car goes east straight through the red. I take a second look, because it's three in the morning, and sure enough it's green for my direction, which means the vehicle went through the red.

I activate my lights and make a right turn onto the avenue and pull in behind the Ford Escape.

The lone driver of the Ford pulls over to the curb, and I call in the plate.

While I'm waiting for the plate to come back, I watch the driver.

The lone driver undoes his seat belt, and the next thing I see is him ducking down.

I wonder, "What in the hell is this guy up to?"

The driver suddenly appears on the passenger side of the vehicle, and puts on his seatbelt.

No one else is in the car, and no one gets out of the car. I almost burst out laughing.

I exit my PC, approach the passenger side of the vehicle, and open the passenger door.

"Well, you fooled me," I say sarcastically.

He turns to me with an idiotic drunken look on his face and says, "I wasn't driving!"

I told him, "No one got out of the car, sir."

"I wasn't driving" he replied in his best drunken slur, at which point I arrested him for impaired driving.

The trial was interesting, especially when the accused tried that defence after I told the judge my story. Guilty was the outcome.

THE VOICE FROM THE CROWD

"11-80, 11-20, 11-50 respond to a large fight at the Parkside Inn."

I look at my watch. It's 2:00 a.m. on a Saturday night. I think *Right on time; the drunks are just being kicked out of the bar.*

I respond, "11-80 to Base, Roger, I'm two minutes away."

The other units also chime in and put themselves en route.

When I pull into the parking lot, I don't see anyone fighting but I do see 11-20 pull in behind my PC (police car).

My first thought is, *crap its 11-20, Dwayne, he's old and very lazy, I hope 11-50 gets here soon.*

We both park our PC's beside the wall leading into the bar.

The bar in this case is actually in the basement, and it has a long set of stairs leading down to the entrance of the bar.

As I get out of the car, I glance back at Dwayne and notice he's taking his time getting out to help.

I walk around the corner of the wall to the set of stairs and look down. There's a large crowd at the bottom of the stairs, and I can see two guys going at it. They are beating the crap out of each other, and the crowd is egging it on.

As I'm waiting for Dwayne to come around the corner, I hear a voice out of the crowd say, "Look out he's got a knife!"

My eyes catch some movement off to my right; I turn my head and a knife is coming toward my side.

I don't have time to think, I just react.

I pivot on my heels and turn, grabbing the wrist of the 16-year-old kid who is trying to stab me. I twist his wrist and he drops the knife. I bend his arm, turning him around, and yell at him as I handcuff him, "I could have shot you, if I had one more second, I could have shot you! Why are you trying to stab me?"

"I didn't want my friend to go to jail for fighting!"

"Are you fucking kidding me, you are going to stab a police officer because you don't want your friend to go to the drunk tank?"

The kid doesn't say anything.

I pick up the knife.

Dwayne then walks around the corner with a puzzled look on his face, wondering why I have this kid in handcuffs in one hand, a knife in my other hand, and I'm walking him to my PC.

Youths, they are barely able to make right decisions and often make wrong ones that could cost them their lives, and in this case mine. Kill a cop because you don't want your buddy to go to the drunk tank. Wow is that a screwed-up decision!

THE RIDE ALONG

I have no problem having a ride-along. I find its a good chance to show the general public a taste of what it's like to be a cop.

On this busy Friday night, I have a young kid who's 18 years old and interested in a policing career and is a friend of one of the inspectors, so here he is on his "ride-along."

The call comes in that there's a noisy party at a house to which I've been called to many times before.

"11-80 to Base, you can cancel the backup on this call, I've got a ride-along and I think we can handle a noise complaint."

"Roger, 11-80, the address is on your MDT (mobile data terminal)."

You could hear the noise a half a block away: loud music, people yelling. A typical party.

"Well, my young friend, let's go have a word with the partiers and tell them to quiet it down, so the neighbours can sleep."

We exit the PC and walk around to the back door, because I've been here a dozen times before and know the front door is blocked off.

Using my flashlight, I knock on the door numerous times before someone comes to open it.

When the door opens, there's a native male with a beer in one hand and an 8-inch kitchen knife sticking out of the middle of his chest. The knife is imbedded almost to the hilt.

The male says, "What do you want?"

The ride-along looks at the knife sticking out of this guy's chest and lets out a high-pitched scream and a "Holy Fuck!"

I grab my radio, "11-80 to Base, I need some backup here and an ambulance. I've got a male with a large knife sticking out of his chest, he's breathing and conscious."

"Sir, let's get you sitting down until the ambulance get here," I say, and I guide him to a kitchen chair.

My ride-along is freaked out and sticks beside me like glue.

The male keeps drinking his beer while sitting in the chair and says, "I'm going to pull this out."

"No, you may bleed to death," I reply, and I grab a towel that is lying on the table. For the first time in my years of service, I do a donut bandage.

I place the donut bandage over the knife and put the male's hand on it and say, "Keep pressure on this. Who stabbed you?"

"I'm not telling you," he replies, taking a swig of his beer.

I look at my ride-along and he's grey and looks like he's going to faint, so I get him to sit down.

My backup arrives, and I get them trying to find out who stabbed this guy, while I wait for the paramedics.

Once the paramedics arrive they look at the victim and say, "Nice donut bandage," and they go about treating him.

The male survived with so many stitches in his chest that he looked like he'd had an autopsy.

The investigation showed the male was trying to "fool around" with a female at the party and his wife didn't like it so, she took the kitchen knife and stabbed him in the chest, and they kept on drinking at the party.

My ride-along decided to choose another career. Apparently, policing is not for everyone.

SHE PLEADED GUILTY

All police officers know that people are strange. People do the weirdest things when they are drunk, high, angry, or all three.

I'm driving the police van on a night shift and I note a Firebird driving erratically so I pull the vehicle over and arrest the driver for impaired driving. The driver is a female escort who is well known to me. I will call her Laura, and she was quite pissed at being arrested.

I drive Laura to the station and put her in the interview room.

I say, "Laura, I will find a female officer to search you."

She replies, "You want to search me? Screw you and your female cop!" She takes off her top and pulls down her pants to show me she has no weapons.

"Laura, put your clothes back on," I say, and I leave the room. Upon returning with a female officer, I open the door and find Laura has pissed in the corner of the room. She says, "Now you have to clean it up," and starts laughing.

I close the door, get a mop and give it to Laura and say, "Here you go." She sees the look on my face and cleans it up.

Laura blows extremely high on the breathalyzer and I see she is too drunk to serve documents to. I decide to transport her to the jail for service in the morning.

It's a busy night. At that time, we could transport males and females in the van, as long as they were all handcuffed. So, I pull the van around and go to load her into the back. Laura looks at the passed-out person on the floor and doesn't want to go into the van.

I advise her, "We don't have private cab service," and made sure she is handcuffed, and put her in the van.

When we arrived at the jail, I open the back of the van and find Laura pulling up her pants, and a large pile of shit on the chest of the passed-out male.

"Are you friggin' kidding me Laura, now you have another charge!"

"I told you not to put me in the back with anyone," she replies.

I haul Laura out and clean up the shit. The passed-out guy doesn't even wake up.

A few months later Laura pleads not guilty to the impaired driving charge, and I meet her in the courthouse.

"Laura, I'm glad you pled not guilty. I can't wait to tell the judge about you pissing in the room and crapping on the passed-out guy."

She changed her plea.

I BLEW IT

It is close to lunch on a warm summer's day. I pull my old Chevy into the Boy Scouts of Canada parking lot to drop off a bag lunch for my wife.

As I walk around the truck, a man appeared out of nowhere. I didn't see him as I pulled in. I usually notice that kind of stuff. The man is older, in his 60's with light coloured hair and deep blue eyes. He is dressed in old jeans and a t-shirt that's a little dirty.

The man asks, "Do you know anywhere I can get some food? I'm hungry but I have no money." He appears embarrassed for asking the question.

The bag lunch comes to mind, *no, my wife needs it.*

I say to the man, "No my friend, but do you see that building at the edge of the parking lot? A friend of mine named Wayne runs the restaurant, and he's always looking for dishwashers. I'm sure if you knock on the door, and tell him Randy sent you, he will give you some work for some food."

I turn away from him, take maybe two steps, and then think, *I should give him the bag lunch. I'll take my wife out to lunch.*

I turn around to give him the lunch, but he is gone. My mind is reeling. I'm muddled, he couldn't be gone, he couldn't have gotten more than ten feet away. Confused, I start looking around, but there's nothing. *What the hell is this??* I look in my truck, under the truck and in the back of the truck. Nothing.

What the hell is going on? I've been a police officer a long time. There's no way someone is getting away from me that quickly, I know how to look for people! I'm angry, astonished and confused. *Where did he go?*

Standing in a nearly empty parking lot, I'm wonder if I'm losing my mind, then clarity of thought comes to me.

I'd been tested. I'd been tested, and I'd failed. An incredible wave of disappointment swept over me. I felt like the lowest thing on the planet.

But then, I realized I'd been tested. I blew it, but I'd been tested!

My eyes focused on the heavens, and my words pour forth, "Sorry God, I blew it this time, but I won't blow it the next time. Thank you!" A wave of joy and excitement flowed though me and I start to laugh.

Walking into my wife's office, I tried to explain to her what had happened. We both went out to the lot and look around. "This is where I was, and there is no way anyone could have gotten away from me that quickly."

I'm not sure who or what he was, but I hope the next time I pass the test instead of blowing it!

INSTINCT

What the hell is that driver doing! He's reaching under the driver's seat like he is reaching for something, but I have no idea what he's up to.

I activate my lights and siren. He glances back in the rear-view mirror as he weaves back and forth in the lane, still reaching under the seat. Finally, he pulls to the curb.

You could tell he was drunk from his driving pattern. He'd crossed the center line several times as I followed him north on the roadway.

Pulling behind him, I angle my PC so the engine is between him and I. His vehicle matched the description of the complainant: an older green Chrysler 300 with one occupant.

My body is tense. Ready to react I watch his every move as I sit in my front seat, my hand on the driver's door in case I must exit quickly. What the hell is he reaching for? My "Spidey sense" is tingling. This guy is up to something. I'm going to call for backup.

"Base this is 11-11, send me a backup unit ASAP."

11-80 responds over the radio, "I'm two blocks away Base, I'm en route."

Staying in my vehicle, I open my driver's door in case he gets out with a weapon. He stays in his vehicle. Good. I hate it when they get out and start walking back toward me. That makes every cop I know very nervous.

Looking in my rear-view mirror, I see the blue and reds appear. I can hear the roar of the powerful police engine. My backup is here.

11-80 pulls his PC behind me, exits and walks up to my door. "What's up?" He says.

"There something wrong with this guy, I'm sure he's the impaired driver the complainant called about."

11-80 says, "You want to go high risk?"

"No, we will just be super cautious. He's up to something."

Getting out of my PC, I approach the driver's door with my hand on my gun. 11-80 at the same time approaches the passenger side of the suspect's vehicle.

He's still trying to reach under the driver's seat and I yell, "Police! Get your hands on the steering wheel!"

The smell of booze pours from the driver's open window and I note a bottle of whisky sitting on the front seat next to him.

He looks at me. His eyes are red, glassy, and bloodshot, but there is something else in his eyes.

I decide that I need to get him under control quickly. Opening the driver's door, I say. "You're under arrest for impaired driving."

I grab his left arm as he is still trying to reach under the seat with his right. He pulls back, my grip locks on his left arm and I pull him out of the vehicle onto the ground.

He keeps resisting, trying to get up, as I get my cuffs out and on his wrists before 11-80 can even get around to the driver's side of the old vehicle.

The guy absolutely reeks of booze and is yelling something we can't make out.

"You're under arrest for impaired driving. I'm going to search you and put you in my vehicle," I say.

Pulling him up off the ground, I start my search. My hand reaches into his jacket pocket and I feel it. I know exactly what it is before I pull my hand out of his pocket. My hand opens to show 11-80. I'm holding six 38 shells.

"Holy Shit!" he says.

"Where's the gun?" I asked, knowing exactly where it is.

"Where's the gun?" I repeat.

The drunken driver replies, "Fuck you cop."

I finish my search of him. Nothing else is found, no gun, no knifes, no identification, so I put him in the back of my PC.

As I walk back to the guy's car, I think I know what he was reaching for. Getting to the driver's side of the vehicle, my hand reaches under the driver seat. The feel of the cold metal is transmitted from my fingertips to my brain.

I try to pull it out, but it feels stuck on something. Bending over I see it. A 38 special, stuck on the springs under the seat. My mouth involuntary utters, "Shit!"

Carefully I push it back from the springs under the seat and pull it out.

11-80 looks down, "Holy Shit, it's cocked back already!"

Releasing the hammer under control, I open the cylinders. Fully cocked and loaded, ready for action. The alarm bells go off in my mind.

"This asshole is lucky he didn't shoot his leg off trying to get this out," I say as I try to use humour to diffuse the seriousness of the situation.

This guy was going to shoot me! Why?

It can happen anytime, anywhere and by anyone, even an old drunk in a green Chrysler.

Thank God for guardian angels.

TRUST

Trust is a tangible thing; you can feel it in your bones. It's not a thought, you know it in your soul, you can take it to the bank as sure as bears shit in the woods (and by the way they do, I've stepped in it!)

In policing, trust is more than the proverbial leap of faith. It's a positive, a no doubt situation.

You must trust yourself and your comrades. Your life depends on it.

I'd been chasing a Dodge pickup for 10 minutes, through lights, alleys, streets and school zones and going high speeds in the residential area at 2 a.m. in the morning.

I wouldn't normally chase this guy, but he just beat and robbed an 82-year-old grandmother for fifty dollars. This asshole was not getting away from me. I got the call and was helping her as he drove by in the Dodge and she said, "That's him."

So, here I am chasing this moron, lights and siren going at 90 km/hour down the street.

"Base, we are going Northbound on 13St at 5 Ave N. Hang on, Base, he not going to make the turn. Base, he just crashed near the Tim Horton at 13 St. Get me an ambulance. Base, He's out of the vehicle running north in the alley. I'm in a foot pursuit."

Panting for breath as I run, I grab my radio, "Base the suspect is a white male in his 20's, black hoody, we are north in the alley."

As I enter the alley the darkness engulfs me. I can see him looking over his shoulder to see how close I'm getting. That's good, because it slows him down, "Stop Police!" I yell, but he speeds up. Typical.

50ft... 30 ft... Shit! He reaches into his hoodie. I run into him like a freight train. I can see the knife in his left hand. I kick him with all my strength in the leg and we fall to the ground, the knife dropping beside him.

He's face down, I've got about 2 seconds. I grab my mike and yell into the radio "10-300, 700 block 13 Street north alley!"

I drop the radio. Now the life struggle continues.

He keeps trying to get the knife. *I've got to stop him.* I get one arm under his neck and the other under his shoulder and flip him away from the knife.

Time slows, like a movie with bad Wi-Fi, my heart is pounding, my breathing sounds like a man gulping water. *I can't let go of this asshole. He's 20 years younger than me, if I do let go, I'm dead.*

My grip tightens, I think, *they're coming, not if they're coming, but when.* The trust is there; it's not faith, it's a certainty.

The guy continues to try and get closer to the knife, but I pull him away. Then I hear it, the sweetest sound in the world: sirens coming closer. I see the red and blues, and hear the tires crunching on the gravel as they throw on the brakes. I hear my brothers' footsteps, and then they are on him. I can relax and breathe.

My trust has been rewarded.

FLYING THE FLAG

It's called "flying the flag." Sitting in front of a hotel in a marked police car, in plain view, hopefully giving the drunks some pause in their stupidity.

They stagger out ready to fight each other, look at the marked unit, realize, "It's the cops," and stumble over to the hotdog guy.

Speaking of the hotdog guy, that's how this tale begins…

Here it is, 2 a.m. on a scorching summer's night. I'm flying the flag outside a downtown hotel when the hotdog guy comes up to my driver's side window.

"Some guy in an old Chrysler just threatened me with a shotgun," he says.

"Did you see the shotgun?" I replied, trying to keep the skepticism out of my voice.

"No, but he went back to the car and I heard some noises and then he drove away, heading downtown."

"Ok, give me a description of him and the car and I'll drive around and see if I can find him."

I start driving around the downtown area thinking, *"The hotdog guy has lost it."* Then I spot a car matching his description: an old green Chrysler with two people in it.

I pull in behind it and activate my lights. The vehicle pulls to the curb.

As I'm running the plate, I see the driver, a female, talking to her male passenger. Actually, they look more like they are yelling at each other.

The plate comes back clean, but I start wondering if I should call in a high-risk takedown. I was thinking, *"No one saw the shotgun, I'll just be super cautious."*

I get out and start walking toward the car and I decide to go to the passenger's window instead of the driver's window just to throw them off a little.

While walking closer to the passenger window, I can see the passenger reaching under the seat for something.

I yell, "Driver and passenger get your hands on the dash, Do it now!"

The driver complies but the passenger keeps reaching under the seat.

My senses go into high alert, my hand rests on the grip of my gun. "Passenger get your hands on the dash! Do it now!"

Reluctantly the male puts his hands on the dash.

I open the passenger door, watching the passenger's hands on the dashboard and I glance down and see the barrel of a shotgun sitting at the passenger's feet.

My gun is in my hand without a thought, and I'm yelling at both of them, "Keep your hands on the dash!"

I hear a noise behind me. It's a male running toward me, he's yelling, "He's got a gun, he wants to kill a cop!"

My thought is, *"How does he know?"*

My attention is split, I need to keep my focus on the gun.

"You stay back, I've got him covered!" I yell.

My left hand leaves my gun and grabs the mike. "Base, 10-300, I need assistance at Fifth Street and Fourth avenue south, I've got two at gunpoint in a vehicle."

The responses hit my earpiece, "11-01 on route, 11-80 on route, 11-40 on route."

In less than minute, two vehicles arrive. The two police officers both exit their vehicles with guns drawn.

"Sam, Neil, get the driver out, I've got the passenger, there's a shotgun at the passenger's feet."

Sam and Neil go to the driver's side of the car, guns squarely pointed at the driver who is in her mid-20's.

Sam holsters his weapon, opens the driver's door, hauls her to the ground, and handcuffs her in what seems like one motion. Sam searches her while she's lying on the ground. Not finding any weapons, he takes her to his PC and returns.

Neil, in the meantime, has shifted his gun focus to the passenger. "Keep your fucking hands on the dash!" he yells.

"Sam, keep me covered, I'll get the passenger."

I holster my gun, grab my cuffs, and put one cuff on his right wrist. I pull on the remaining cuff as a lever to haul his ass to the ground, away from the shotgun.

I cuff him, search him, and throw him in my PC.

I can feel my breath return; the danger is over. The feeling of "Holy Shit!" now engulfs me. I take a second, shake it off.

"Neil, the guy in the parking lot over there apparently saw what happened. Can you get a statement from him?"

Sam approaches me and asks, "What the hell is going on?" I give him the story and we both approach the open passenger door and see the shotgun on the floor.

I haul the shotgun out and find a slug in the barrel and two more in the magazine.

The words, "Holy Fuck!" escape my lips as I realize how close I came.

Neil comes backs and fills me in on the Good Samaritan's story. Apparently about a minute before I pulled over the Chrysler, the vehicle had pulled up in front of him standing in front of the hotel. The male stuck the shotgun out the window, racked it and said, "I'm going to go kill a cop!"

In policing you never know how many times you come close to death, yet at times you do. During the event you stay focused and strong. It's after that your hands tremble.

GOOD MOVE

Working traffic as a police officer is always interesting. You get to meet people, help them in traumatic circumstances like traffic collisions, and you get to chat with them as you either issue them a warning or write them up.

The city was having a lot of problems with trucks being off the truck route and causing traffic issues, so we were asked to keep an eye out for truck route offences.

Driving around in the early morning hours I see a Hutterite grain truck driving way off the truck route in a residential area. I pull him over.

As I hand the ticket to the driver I explained to him, "You can't be off the truck route in this size of vehicle unless you're making a delivery or picking items up."

The man suddenly gets an a-ha moment, and walks away from me with his ticket in hand. He goes to the cab of his truck, grabs a dozen eggs, walks over to a house and rings the doorbell.

This young woman, who obviously just woke up, comes to the door and says "Yes?"

The Hutterite promptly says, "Here's your delivery," and hands the perplexed women the eggs.

He walks back to me smiling. At this point, I start laughing and take the ticket back and say, "Excellent move, very resourceful!"

I voided the ticket and had a great story to tell.

YOUR HURRY

Your hurry caused me to cry.

Your hurry caused me pain.

Your hurry spread, caused my wife pain, caused her to hurt, to cry.

Your hurry travelled across provinces, made my mom weep, my sister call and reach out.

Your hurry made the waitress wonder, "Why is that nice couple crying? Why are their tears flowing into their breakfast?"

Your hurry reached out and united friends and family.

Your hurry hurt his brothers. They held his hands, and they cried and hummed softly to him, as he lay in the midst of a drug-induced coma.

Your hurry hurt, caused a three-month-old baby to cry because she felt the pain in her papa's eyes.

He sleeps in a coma, with a tube helping him to breathe, and another tube feeding him. He hurts, the pain is overwhelming when he awakes, and the machines beep and sound their alarms, and the nurses slowly put him back into the painless abyss.

Most of all your hurry will carry on for years. His body will always remember your hurry, in his battered brain and his crushed leg. In his very breath he remembers, through his broken ribs. When he writes, his hand will remember the shattered fingers. His scarred face carries the mark of your hurry.

Your hurry cost so much.

Was the extra minute worth the pain? The pain spread to his girlfriend, his mom, his dad, his brothers, his grandparents, and the rest of his family and friends. Your minute saved will multiply into years of rehabilitation, therapy and suffering.

Your hurry caused you to lose your integrity, to lie. Your hurry caused you to blame him for his injuries. How dare you!

I hope you remember your hurry; him hitting the front of your car, smashing through your windshield, him flying through the air, his poor head hitting the ground, his knuckles ground entirely off!

Your head remembers.

My son's body remembers, and will always carry the scars of your hurry.

GHOST RIDER

At two in the morning on a night shift, if you're not on a call, it's the prime time to look for impaired drivers.

One-night shift I'm driving my PC north on 13th Street facing a green light, when in front of me a westbound car goes through the red at about 60 km/hour. I noticed a wave of flames flowing from the back of the vehicle.

I shake my head, because I can't believe what I see. Turning the corner to catch up with the vehicle, I see both back tires are on fire!

The sparks are flying thirty feet back as the rims dig into the asphalt.

"Base, I've got a vehicle going north on 5th Ave with the back tires on fire, get the fire department coming my way and I'll let you know where I stop him".

I activate my emergency lights and the vehicle pulls over to the side of the road.

I exit my PC and run up to the driver and open the driver's door. The driver is obviously intoxicated and immediately yells, "Why are you stopping me? I didn't do anything wrong!"

"It might have something to do with your back tires being on fire," I say. I haul him away from the car and arrest him for impaired driving. The guy has no idea his car is fire and then accuses me of starting his car on fire. Drunks!

The fire department arrives a few minutes later and puts the fire out.

I find out later the guy had committed a hit-and-run in a bar parking lot and escaped by jumping the curb, which popped both back tires.

I'll never forget the image of the car, with the wave of flames and sparks flying behind it high in the air looking like the Ghost Rider out of comic books.

THANK YOU

I've met so many people that I can't remember them all. I know I've met them, but the where and the when elude me. I used to remember everyone. Where I met them. Who they were, and even their names. Now I have people that I don't recall coming up to me and saying, "Hi".

I get into conversations with them. I keep it generic, and hope something pops up, as to when and where, and who they are. It usually comes to me after a while, and I can place them.

Most often, when it comes to me, it's because of how they are talking. Their tone says whether I helped them, or if I threw cuffs on them.

If I've helped them, I keep the conversation light and interactive.

If I've thrown cuffs on them, I withdraw a little. I am tenser and more precise about the things I say.

The woman comes up to me at the Christmas party and says, "Aren't you Constable Ward?"

After saying, "Yes," I can feel my guard come up. My wife, who is holding my hand, senses my tension.

I don't recognize the woman as she talks, but I can see tears form and fall from her dark brown eyes. She mouthed the words, "Thank you."

I relax and say, "What for?"

"When my husband was beating me, you tore him off me. I thought I was going to die! You arrested him and got him away from me, but that was just part of it. The words you said to me, struck me, and stayed with me. You said that I didn't deserve this, that it was not my fault, and that I could change my life, and the lives of my children."

"I left him after he went to jail that night, and I remember you driving me and the kids to the shelter. I remember how kind you were to me."

My wife is standing beside me, and I can see her eyes tearing up.

I tried to remember her, but there were so many beaten wives.

The woman touch's my arm and says, "Thanks to you, and the words you said, I started to believe. I wasn't the worthless piece of crap like he said I was. I thought, you were right. I didn't deserve this. It wasn't my fault. My life has changed since that night. I went to school. I got a job, and believe it or not, I work at the police station where I live, and I married a cop."

My mind works to remember her, but all the faces of those poor women have blended together over the years.

The woman again says, "Thank you," and asks if she can hug me.

She hugs me and says, "I'll let you and your lovely wife go back to the party."

When I turn to my wife, her eyes and face radiate with pride and love.

As we start back to our table, my mind is still trying to remember the woman.

My thoughts are, *Words are powerful, but deeds change lives.*

I say a silent prayer and thank God that I was there to help.

At home that night, I awake from a restless sleep, and the woman's face comes to me. I remember the black eye, the red purple marks on her throat, and the four-year-old sitting on her lap, crying, as I drove them to the shelter.

Sleep eluded me as faces of other beaten women comee to me.

I hope my actions, words, and deeds has helped them.

Where are their lives at now?

LEAVE THEM IN THE CAR

It's 10 p.m. on a Friday night.

Normally, the radio would be blaring with calls from dispatch to go here, go there, but tonight nothing. Maybe the stars are aligned. Maybe all the crazies are inside or visiting their mother or something.

Dare I say, or think the "Q" word "Quiet"? You never use that word because when you do you usually regret it; because it then becomes anything but quiet.

"11-11, 11-30 respond to an impaired driver call on the north side, details are on your MDT" (Mobile data terminal).

A couple of minutes later, I'm in the parking lot of the mall where the MDT said the vehicle with the impaired driver was, and lo and behold, there it is. The red Dodge Charger is there, but it has four subjects in it, not one.

Activating my lights, I pull up behind the vehicle. The driver turns around, and I can see the "Oh shit" look on his face.

"Base, I'm out with the vehicle with four occupants."

"11-30 responding as backup, I'll be there in 45 seconds."

Approaching the driver, I shine my light in the back seat and see two subjects who look intoxicated.

The driver rolls down his window. "License and registration please," are my instructions.

The driver has the look. He is pissed; the smell of booze assaults my nose.

79

"Yes, officer," the driver says in his best "drunkese."

Well, I may as well get this show on the road. "Driver, step out of the vehicle. Passengers, stay where you are."

The driver steps out, and I take him by the arm saying, "You're under arrest for impaired driving."

The driver mumbles, "Please, don't do this to me"

Like I'm doing this to him, like I poured the booze down his throat and made him drive his car.

As I'm escorting the driver back to my PC, my backup, 11-30, pulls up.

It's a new police officer. He's only been out on his own maybe 2 months. "Keep an eye on the passengers, I'll take care of the driver," I say.

While starting to handcuff the driver and to put him in the back, I look up to see the rookie's getting the passengers out of the vehicle.

The other drunks start wandering over, telling me, "Let him go."

"Get your asses back in the car!" I reply.

One of the passenger's steps forward and grabs my arm. I knock his hand away.

The driver starts to pull away, but I have one handcuff on his arm. He takes a swing at me with the other arm.

The fight is on! Two of the passenger's step toward me, one takes a swing. I duck under, twist the cuff and the driver goes to the ground.

Looking over, I see the rookie is fighting with the other passenger.

The other two passengers are almost on top of me. One foot goes on the driver who's on the ground, and with my free hand I pull out my baton. The baton makes a loud crack as it expands, but it doesn't stop passenger #1 who kicks at me.

My baton swings downward, hitting the leg.

Passenger # 2 gets behind me and tries to put me in a chokehold.

My mind is reeling, one foot is on the neck of the driver, I have one hand on the handcuff on his arm, the other has a baton in it.

No choice, I keep my foot on the driver's neck and let go of his arm.

Grabbing the arm around my neck, I grind my baton into it, and passenger #2 let's go.

I duck under, grab his arm, and twist it so he has no choice but to fall on top of the driver, who is now trying to get up.

Grabbing my radio, I yell into the mike "11-11 to Base, 10-300, we need backup!"

I start to back up, but one of the assholes on the ground grabs my pant leg. I fall to the ground.

My ground fighting training kicks in: deal with the closest threat.

Passenger #1, who now has an extremely sore leg from my baton strike, jumps on me. Two hits in the face, and he's down for now.

Passenger #2 now has my attention as he's gotten off the driver and is trying to grab onto me. My baton swings around hitting him right on his forearm.

This is an all-out fight for my life.

Arms try to grab me, I kick out or hit them with my baton. I need to get my ass off the ground before all three come at me at once.

I hit one of the guys trying to grab me in the face, his nose explodes in an eruption of blood all over me.

Minutes go by. I'm getting tired, but so are they.

Finally, I manage to get up. I get my back to the PC and I hear it, the sweetest sound in the world, sirens.

I have a second, the rookie has his guy on the ground cuffed, his shirt is ripped, there's blood all over his face, but he's holding his own.

Passenger #1 is yelling and limping toward me again. I hit him in the leg with the baton. He piles into the driver and they both fall to the ground in a heap.

Passenger #2 is out, lying on the ground holding his bloody nose.

Quickly, I jump on top of passenger #1, who's on top of the driver. I hold them both there until the cavalry arrives.

The hard braking into the parking lot, hands grabbing onto the assholes, sinks into my consciousness.

I can rest; the breaths come deep and long as I let my comrades take over.

After a minute, I see the rookie lying on the ground leaning against his car, catching his breath. Walking over, I see he's got a black eye, blood all over him. He looks a mess, but he'll live.

Bending down, I look him square in the face and say, "Leave them in the car."

I stand up and walk away to deal with the consequences from the rookie's mistake.

$20 AND TWO CHICKENS

You come across a lot of things walking downtown instead of being in your Police Car. You interact a lot more, you chat a lot more, and people get to know you.

The difficulty arises when you come across things you wouldn't normally write a ticket for, but the public sees you and you must do something.

Take for instance the time when I'm walking down 3rd Avenue in the heart of downtown, when lo and behold a Hutterite man jaywalks across the street, 50 feet from the crosswalk, stopping traffic.

Well, the horns start blowing, and several drivers look at me walking downtown in uniform looking for a crime to solve. They point to the Hutterite.

Something needs to be done, so I call the Hutterite over to have a chat.

I decide to write this guy up. As I hand him the ticket, he sees the amount, and he yells in his best Hutterite accent, "Wow, that's expensive, can you reduce it? Can you make it $20 and two chickens?"

"Well, I don't think the judge will go for that" I reply, trying not to laugh because he is serious. "How about $20 and three chickens?" he asks.

I quickly explained to him there is no place on the ticket to write down chickens and that the courts prefer cash. He goes away mumbling about the cost of the ticket.

Life does get more interesting when you shed your steel skin of a police vehicle and interact with the public.

THE KNOCK

How many times have I been the knock at the door?

The informer of change.

When I knock, their life is never the same. It may come back, but it's never the same.

They always think back to the knock on the door.

The hesitant look, their mind trying to grasp, *why?*

Why is that policeman knocking on my door with the sad look on his face?

They open, not wanting to, but they must know.

The news is never good when I knock on the door.

I wish I could bring good news, news of a birth, news of a life saved, rather than a life taken or injured.

The knock comes to all, in one form or another, a policeman, a clergyman, a mother, daughter, father or son.

The knock that comes changes lives forever.

LIGHTNING SPEED

Knife attacks are usually extremely quick and extremely violent.

I was dispatched to the park for an intoxicated subject on a park bench. When I arrive, I recognize him as a regular customer, and feel comfortable in waking him up without cuffing him first.

"You wake up!" I say, kicking the bottom of his feet to give him a stir.

The guy opens his eyes, and yells, "Fuck you cop!"

My senses go up in a hurry, and I'm ready for almost anything, except this.

The guy reaches, well, or starts to reach, for a knife in his boot.

I see him move, but due to his intoxicated state, he's literally moving at about quarter speed. I mean, he's in slow motion! His hand is moving so slow that I can probably run back to my police car by the time his hand gets to his boot, or at least run around the park bench a few times.

I start laughing. As his hand finally gets to his boot and is pulling out the knife, I grab his arm and twist it slightly, causing him to drop the knife.

I cannot stop laughing as I put the handcuffs on him.

He says, "What are you laughing at?"

"Your lightning speed, my friend," and I haul him off to jail.

THE WRONG WAY NAKED LADY STOP

The advantage of driving the police van is that you're up higher. There is maybe one other advantage in that you have a little more room in the cab. The disadvantages are that it's slower, clumsy, people can see you coming a lot sooner, and it's just uncomfortable to drive.

On a night shift in the summer, I'm driving the van at 3:00 a.m. going down a one-way road. I suddenly see a vehicle coming at me, going the wrong way.

I activate my lights, and the vehicle slows down and stops about 50 feet in front of me. There is nowhere for the female driver to go, she has to stop, as there are boulevards on both sides which would take some effort to drive over.

I activate my front spot light and it shines inside the vehicle. I can see the female driver's head bow down. It looks like she is starting to cry.

I get out cautiously and approach the driver's side of the vehicle.

As I get close, I can definitely see she is crying and naked!

I'm thinking, *who drives her car at three in the morning naked, going the wrong way down a one-way?*

I tap on the window, and she lowers the driver's window.

"I can see you don't have a weapon or a driver's license on you, so I am going back to my van and you can put the clothes on I see piled up in the back seat."

I go back to my van while she gets dressed. I am taking a chance that she doesn't come out with a weapon, but in policing you make and take those chances.

After a minute or two, I come back to the driver's open window. She is still sobbing but at least she has some clothes on.

After getting her license and insurance, I say, "Ok, miss, what's up with the naked driving at three in the morning, and why are you going the wrong way on a one-way?"

Sobbing and practically yelling she says, "Please don't give me a ticket, please don't. My husband will find out I was cheating on him. My boyfriend works at the convenience store two blocks away and after we made out, I just jumped in my car to go home, and it was easier for me to go the wrong way for the two blocks than to go down to the intersection and turn around. Please don't arrest me, don't give me a ticket."

In policing you make big decisions that affect people's lives, and small ones that also can have a tremendous effect on their lives.

The question is, do you give her a ticket, and what effects will that have on her family, all because she decided to cheat on her husband, and drive the wrong way on a one-way?

Well, I didn't issue a ticket and I wonder if the husband was awake when she got home. If so, what excuse did she give for being out at three in the morning?

Well, I know we didn't get a domestic call after that, so I guess it worked out to some degree for her.

I didn't give any names, but I did have to share with my fellow cops, the wrong way naked lady story.

I had to put up with them saying, "You should have called me for backup." Well that's just not me, but it was a great stop to share.

You never know what the next stop will be.

MENTAL ILLNESS

Police officers have lots of experience dealing with mental illness. We experience the effects first hand. We see the effects on the person who has the mental illness, on their family and friends, and on the police officers and emergency personnel attending the call. We often deny the effects they have on us as police officers and emergency personnel.

The people with mental illness often don't think about the effect they have on the cops that show up at the calls they generate. Now just to clarify, I know they are not thinking properly, so I'm not blaming, I'm just stating a fact. Some people with mental illness do think about the effects they have on the cops, and due to their mental illness, revel in the fact of the pain they will cause cops.

An example: we got a call for a suicidal male on the bridge. My partners and I arrive at the different ends of the bridge. We ensure that the trains are stopped, and we walk from each end of the bridge until we come across the suicidal male.

When you're dealing with a suicidal person one of the first things to try and do is to open a dialogue.

In this case the male is on the edge of the railing, sitting down and for some reason has a length of barbed wire in his hand.

My partner does a great job connecting with the guy and manages to talk him out of jumping. We approach him and arrest him under the Mental Health Act.

When we have him in handcuffs and are in the process of taking him to the hospital, I ask him, "What was the barbed wire for?"

He gets this excited look on his face and says, "I was going to put it around my neck, tie the other end to the bridge and when I jumped, it would rip my head off. The cops would arrive and would just find the head dangling in the wind!" Then he laughed.

I realize that this is the mental illness talking, but I still get angry inside because I know how that would have affected the cop who showed up at that scene.

Waking up in the middle of the night, seeing the scene in your head. Trying to go back to sleep and not waking your partner next to you. Being reminded of it, every time you come to the bridge again, or see barbed wire sitting on a store shelf or fence. The counselling, the talks with other cops, and the pain and loss of faith in humanity.

Police and other emergency personnel see and feel the effects of other's decisions, both the good decisions they make and the bad decisions they make.

DEATH ON THE FRONT DOORSTEP

The daughter and her boyfriend showed up at her mother's front door around 8 a.m. and found her. The 911 call came as a 10-60 (Death) in the front yard.

I'm working the zone, so the call comes to me. When I arrive, the paramedics are still en route. I go up to the front door where a 45-year-old female is dead lying face down on the front step. Her housecoat is pulled up; she is not wearing panties, exposing everything below her breasts. The signs of death are obvious. Rigour mortis has set in. Her face is frozen in death and her eyes are wide open.

This is not a normal death; this appears to possibly be a sexual assault and death.

"11-60 to Base, I need a supervisor, forensics, and detectives at this location. At this point the 10-60 appears to be not natural. I need additional units to secure the scene."

"Base to 11-60, roger 11-01 (Supervisor), Forensics is en route, CID (Criminal Investigation Division) has been notified and the Homicide Unit will be en route shortly."

Backup arrives shortly. I have them secure the perimeter while I clear the scene, secure the witnesses and the body.

I've worked at numerous deaths scenes and know the investigation procedure of Body, Scene, and History. All that must be in sync for the death to be deemed natural. In the preliminary stages of this investigation, things appear to be not natural.

I've secured the witnesses for the history portion. Upon examining the scene, one of the first oddities is, how did her housecoat get pulled up? There are no signs of trauma, no blood or contusions. Rigour mortis indicates the body has not been moved, as the blood is pooled inside the body, making bruises where her body touches the deck surfaces.

One of the puzzling things that strikes me is, the paper was delivered. The paper arrives about 6 a.m., but the call did not come in until 8 a.m.: that did not make sense. It is clear the body has been out here all night. Why didn't the call come when the paper was delivered?

When the detectives arrive, I brief them on my findings and leave them to their scene and body examinations, while I look at the history portion of this death investigation.

I approach the daughter and her boyfriend. She is sitting on the couch not crying, which is unusual.

"Miss, I'm sorry for your loss," and I introduce myself.

"I'm sorry I need to confirm this, is that your mother on the front step?"

"Yes," she says angrily.

"Tell me about your mother and her medical history as best you can, and how you found her."

The young 17-year-old goes into the night's events and into her mom's history with drugs.

The young girl had spent the night at her boyfriend's and found her mother at 8 a.m. on the front doorstep, as reported. The husband is rock climbing in the states and she has informed him of the death. He will be coming back to Canada when he gets down from the mountain.

The history portion of death investigations is where you not only find out about the medical history, but also the relationship history of the deceased. You find out about how she related to her husband, her siblings, her neighbours, her friends and who saw her last.

The daughter tells the story of a loving mother and father who were traveling up north for a vacation in their new truck, four years ago. Their truck goes across some railroad tracks but due to a mechanical fault in the truck design, the steering wheel came down on her father's lap and he lost control of the vehicle, rolling the truck several times.

Both survived the accident, but the mother had a broken back and spent months in the hospital taking pain medications. The mother got addicted to pain meds and changed from a loving mother to a drug addict.

The daughter goes on to say her mom went to treatment but couldn't beat the drugs. She would steal drugs from her father's office, who was in the medical profession.

I can see the love on the daughter's face when she speaks about her mother before the accident, and their change of relationship after the accident. The daughter is angry with her mom for being addicted to drugs, for the person she had become. She ends with the fact that she knew one day she would come home and her mother would be dead from an overdose.

I examine the house and note pictures of a loving family together, and think about how one moment changed their lives, how things are related. How a fault in a truck design led to a woman's death on the front steps. Choices were made, that led to that death, but you still must look at those pivotal moments in life that effect all others, that change the course of what could have been, to what it is.

The detectives come in and I give them my report. They report that no signs of foul play were observed on the body, but it will be sent for autopsy.

I continue my portion of the investigation by going to talk to the 12-year-old paperboy who delivered the paper at the house.

I speak to the parents of the paperboy. I let them know what happened and ask permission to talk to their son.

"You were out delivering papers this morning. Anything unusual happen on your route this morning?'

"Nope," says the boy.

"Nothing out of place?"

"Well there was a mannequin laying on the front step of a house."

Now I knew. The boy doesn't know death. His mind said it was a mannequin, so he delivered the paper and went on his way.

I leave him with his version of reality as it made no sense to change it.

After weeks, the autopsy finds no sexual assault. The cause of death was a drug overdose and manner of death was an accidental overdose.

For me, this particular death, always reminded me of how fragile life is, of how one moment can change your life and the lives of others forever.

NOT TODAY

The call comes in as a teenage male heading to the bridge to commit suicide.

"11-80 to Base, I'll take the westside and walk east."

"11-30 to Base, I'll take the eastside and walk west."

I head over to the westside and park my car in the normal spot, because I'd been through numerous calls of people wanting to kill themselves on this bridge.

The last call we had the jumper didn't go far enough onto the bridge to die instantly. When he jumped he didn't die right away, we found him in the morning with two broken legs, and you could see how far he crawled injured, and where he died.

Back to the bridge.

As I walk across east towards the other units walking west, I glanced at the open rails and the river bottom hundreds of meters below.

The radio squeals, "11-30 to Base, I can see a figure on the middle of the bridge, please confirm all trains are stopped."

Base replies, "Units on the bridge, CP rail has confirmed all trains are stopped."

I see the figure in the middle of the bridge. It looks to be a male, but I'm still hundreds of meters off and I can't tell for sure yet.

As we get closer, I confirm it's a male sitting on the edge of the railing, but it's not a teenager, it's middle-aged man.

"Base, confirm we are looking for a 17-year-old suicidal youth."

"Roger 11-80, we were looking for a 17-year-old youth, but we just got the call from the complainant that he's at home."

Well, who the hell is this guy, and what's he doing on the bridge?

As we get close to the guy, my partner opens the discussion and talks to him about suicide and jumping from the bridge.

The guy says he came to the bridge to jump off, and that he didn't let anyone know. He's wondering how we knew he was on the bridge?

My partner says, "Someone doesn't want you to die. Look, we didn't know you were here. We got a call about a young male who was going to jump, but it ended up he's at home now. It's obvious someone is looking out for you. We are here to help you, the big guy brought us here, and we don't want you to die, that's the only explanation."

The guy gets a puzzled look on his face, and takes out a bullet from his pocket.

He says, "Earlier today, I tried to kill myself with my rifle, but when I pulled the trigger it wouldn't go off, so I took the bullet out and came to the bridge."

I say, "Are you kidding me? You tried to kill yourself with a gun today, the bullet didn't work, and now you come to the bridge to jump off! You didn't let anyone know, and we show up here. Someone doesn't want you to die. You have something you are meant to do in life, my friend. You are meant to live today."

The guy's face lightens up, and he gets down and comes closer to us.

"I think you are right."

My partner arrests him under the Mental Health Act and we take him to the hospital.

My thoughts swirled around, amazed at the way life works. If we hadn't gotten that call about the suicidal youth, we wouldn't have been on the bridge, and this guy would have jumped. The guy tried to kill himself earlier and the bullet didn't work. I looked at the bullet; it had firing pin marks on it.

Wow, someone really didn't want this guy to die today!

THE SHOES

One of the responsibilities of a police officer is to be a truth finder.

The call comes in as a break and enter (B&E), sexual assault. More information comes across the radio as other units head to the scene.

Dispatch reports, "Units responding to the B&E, sexual assault call, the woman advises she stabbed the suspect with a kitchen knife, and he's bleeding on the stairway."

"11-80 roger."

"11-20 roger."

I'm the acting sergeant that night, so I say, "11-01 on route, make sure the paramedics stage but tell them not to enter until we secure the scene."

Dispatch responds, "Roger, 11-01."

The complainant lives in a basement suite. When my guys arrive, they have to kick in the locked door leading to the basement suite.

When I arrive, they are handcuffing the suspect, who is laying on the basement stairs bleeding and semi-conscious from blood loss. The complainant is yelling and crying near the bottom of the stairs.

I look at the kicked in door and at the top of the landing is a set of men's white running shoes. I look down at the guy laying on the stairs and noticed he does not have any shoes on.

Odd, I think. *Who breaks into a house to sexually assault someone, takes their shoes off and puts them neatly at the top of the stairs?*

The scene is secured, so I call the paramedics up. They have to transport him to hospital. I have 11-20 go in the ambulance with him, so we can have continuity.

11-80 is an experienced officer and is trying to calm the victim down to find out what happened.

The woman refuses to come to the station and is uncooperative to a large degree. This raises a red flag with me.

The woman says she had been at the bar, came home about an hour before and had sent home the babysitter who had been watching her 6-month-old son, who was asleep in the bedroom. She reports that the guy entered the house about an hour after she got home and tried to sexually assault her. The woman sticks to her story for over an hour.

Things didn't make sense, but at this point we had to be careful. Until you have the evidence, or a reasonable suspicion, you don't want to accuse a sexual assault "victim" of lying.

The woman states she stabbed the guy when she encountered him in the living room, but the only blood is on the stairs. The door was locked when my guys arrived at the scene and they had to kick it in. *Who takes their shoes off at a B&E?*

I call in the forensics team and they confirm my suspicions that the guy was stabbed on the stairs.

To this point, the guy who was stabbed is in surgery and can't answer any questions. But after about an hour and a half, the guy was out of surgery, and 11-20 has a chance to question him.

11-20 calls me on the telephone. "Boss, the guy says he was at the bar and was trying to pick up some good-looking women. When he couldn't, he decided to try for our victim, who he thought was a little chunky. He started making out with her at the bar and got the girl's address. When she left the bar, he took a taxi to her address. He says she let him in, and they started making out. After a few minutes he got a text from a better-looking girl and decided to leave. The girl got pissed and stabbed him when he was walking up the stairs." 11-20 continued, "The guy's a jerk boss, but I think he's telling the truth."

I say, "Can you ask him what kind of shoes he was wearing?"

11-20 says, "White runners, and they are at the top of the stairs."

My guys check with the taxi company and the bar and the guy's story is confirmed.

Now, I have reasonable suspicion that the woman is lying. She is advised that she will be charged with aggravated assault, mischief and other charges. She is advised of her rights and caution.

The woman admitted to stabbing the guy after I confronted her with the shoes, the locked door, the taxi and information from the bar.

She says, "I stabbed that asshole because he was leaving for another prettier girl."

The job of the police is to find the truth, to have enough evidence to convict the guilty, and to exonerate the innocent.

Sometimes that process takes a while. Sometimes it even means exonerating assholes.

HOW YOU DOING?

Calls to bars can be quite dangerous. You're in a crowed place. Patrons of the bar sometimes throw bottles at you or try to grab at your gun because they think it's funny, I guess.

The call came in as a disturbance inside the bar. My partner and I arrive in separate police cars at about the same time.

As we are going into the bar, I grab one of the bouncers to show us where the disturbance is. I always bring one of the employees with me to keep an eye on our backs.

We nudge our way through the throngs of people still gyrating to the music and reach the far corner of the bar.

One guy is kneeling on the floor of the bar screaming and crying his eyes out. A few feet away, an attractive girl stands near a table with a bouncer who has one arm hanging onto her, so she can't leave.

I go up to the bouncer hanging onto the girl and say, "What happened?"

He brings up his other arm, which is holding a can of pepper spray and says, "She sprayed him."

I turn to the girl and say, "Why did you spray him?"

"He was hitting on me."

"You sprayed him with pepper spray because he was hitting on you?"

"Yea, I didn't want him hitting on me."

"How was he hitting on you?"

"He came up and said, "How you doing?", so I sprayed him."

The "hitter's" eyes were quickly washed out and the young lady was charged with assault with a weapon, possession of a prohibited weapon, plus a few other things and was taken to the station.

I'm always amazed at the stupidity of people sometimes, and how they justify their actions. The girl truly thought she was justified in spraying someone because he was hitting on her, in a bar!

DRUNKS MAKE BAD DECISIONS

While flying the flag outside of the bar at two in the morning you see some strange things.

You hope that having a marked police car parked, where all the drunks can see it will deter them from stupidity. Maybe that's true for some, but not for all.

On this night, my marked police car is parked near the bar. I see this vehicle going slowly down the alley behind the bar, and as it exits the alley it goes in the wrong direction facing traffic.

My sharp police instincts kick in, and I know this guy has to be pissed. Apparently, the driver finally realizes he's going the wrong way, and gets back into the correct lane.

I pull my vehicle behind him and activate the emergency equipment. The driver pulls over, and I get out and approach the vehicle, and its two occupants, one driver and one passenger.

"License and registration please," I say. The smell of booze reeks from the driver and I know I am going to arrest him for impaired driving. When I look down and see an IID (ignition interlocking device). It's essentially a breathalyzer that requires the driver to blow into it before starting his vehicle. If the driver has alcohol on his breath, the vehicle will not start.

I'm thinking, *how did this driver get the car started, he's pissed as a nit.*

I arrest the driver for impaired driving, and after cautioning him, I ask him. "How did you get your car started with the IID?"

He replies, "My passenger is sober, so he blew into the machine."

"If he's sober why didn't you let him drive, when you knew you were drunk?" I say.

He turns to me with a defiant look and says, "No one but me drives my car!"

"Are you friggin' kidding me? You're drunk, you have a sober person in the car who can drive, you get him to blow into the machine rather than let him drive, all because you have some idiot rule that no one else drives your car?" I say.

He looks at me with his drunken stare and doesn't say a word.

I tow his car away and take him to the station for the breathalyzer, which by the way, he blew way over the legal limit.

Drunks make bad decisions.

DON'T LET NAKED PEOPLE INTO YOUR HOUSE

Night shift is when interesting things usually happen. Dayshift is when things pop up that you didn't find on the nightshift.

On this cold winter's night, the call comes in around three in the morning about a naked man running down the middle of the street yelling. I normally try to avoid naked men calls, but I head to the area. Prior to arriving in the area, dispatch advises that a lady has let the naked man into her house, and that we should proceed to that address.

I think: *Who lets naked people into their house at three in the morning?*

Upon arriving at the house, we discover that the lady indeed has let the naked man in and has given him a blanket.

I look at the naked man, and using my keen sense of humour say, "Cold out tonight." I wasn't sure if he caught the shrinkage joke.

I speak to the lady and advise her it was unwise to let naked or unknown clothed people into her house at any time of the day.

I take the guy to my police car, get him a better blanket and turn up the heat, while I chat with him about why he was running naked down the street with only running shoes on.

Apparently, the guy had been at a hot tub party about seven blocks north of our current location, and he got dared to run around the block naked. Well, being as drunk as he was he accepted the challenge but got lost in the process.

I manage to get a rough location as to where the hot tub party is and decide to drive him back rather than hauling his naked butt to the drunk tank.

When I pull up in front of the house there are partygoers and another drunk who has a small German Shepherd pup on a leash. The pup is maybe three months old.

German Shepherd guy has the naked guy's underwear, and is pushing it in the pup's nose, saying in his best drunken slur, "Go find him." The pup wanted nothing to do with the stinky underwear and keeps turning his head and sneezing.

My partner and I start laughing our faces off and hand the naked guy over to the partygoers, so they can put him in the hot tub to warm up.

The best advice I have for people is this: Don't let naked people into your house in the middle of the night. Don't run naked around the block. And dogs need to be trained to track and not be a puppy.

DON'T PRAY FOR PATIENCE

I found that after a few years of policing I was getting impatient with people. Instead of saying, "Get over here," I would say, "GET OVER HERE!"

I didn't like that person, so I did something about it.

After a Bible Study one night I went to my pastor, and we prayed for patience.

The next day after the Bible Study, my partners and I get a call to a stabbing at an apartment.

When I arrive, I find the "victim" of the stabbing is being held on the floor of the apartment by neighbours who heard the domestic incident. I recognize the guy on the floor as an extremely violent individual I'd dealt with in the past.

Apparently, the stabbing "victim" was beating up on his girlfriend in the apartment because she didn't want to go hooking for him anymore. The girl was getting so badly beaten, that she reached up on the kitchen counter, grabbed a pair of scissors, and stabbed him in the upper thigh. He kept beating on her until the neighbours came in and stopped the beating, holding him until I arrived.

I cuff the stabbing "victim," and take him to my police van while my partners take care of the girl.

I am purposefully trying to practice my patience with this guy, and I gently put him in the back of police van. I call for an ambulance, but it's a busy day and they are taking a while, so I advise dispatch I am transporting him to the hospital.

When I arrive at the hospital, nurses are waiting in the bay with a wheelchair.

I open the back of the van, and I gently help this guy down the van stairs, when he spits on the side of my face. Now this isn't just spittle, it's green disgusting mucus.

I don't know if any of you have had the experience someone spitting on you, but it is one of the most humiliating things one human being can do to another. You would think I'd be angry, but for some reason it doesn't bother me at all. I gently take him down the van stairs and put him in the wheelchair.

I can't say the same for the nurses. They are extremely upset with the guy. So much so, they start yelling at the guy and telling him how disgusting that was.

I continue into the hospital and lay the guy on a gurney, and he kicks at me, and tries to spit at me, so I put a mask on him.

The guy connects with a kick on my upper arm, so I hobble his feet and charge him with assault on a Peace Officer.

After I take him to the jail, I head back to the station to fill out the paperwork. As I talk to my fellow cops about this guy spitting on me, I start getting angry. The more I talk to other cops about this guy spiting on me, the angrier I get. I am angrier than I've ever been. I am seething, I've never been as angry as I was when I finished that shift.

My wife realizes something is wrong. I'm a talkative person, but for days I hardly said a word.

At the next Bible study, my pastor comes up to me and says, "What's wrong? You're not usually this quiet."

I tell him the story and we pray about it. After a few days I feel better.

I can say that I haven't always been as patient with people who have spit on me since that incident.

I'm telling you this story because people are always watching you. What you do, and how you do it influences others.

A few months after this spitting incident, I again am in the hospital with a guy that has been stabbed, when a nurse comes up to me and says, "I know you."

I reply, "I'm in here all the time."

"Yes, but you're so patient with assholes. That guy spit on the side of your face and you did nothing! You were so patient with him and all I wanted to do was slap him upside his disgusting face. How did you stay so patient with him?" she said.

I tell her the whole story and advise her to never pray for patience, because you'll get a chance to practice it.

COLUMBINE CHANGED EVERYTHING

The Columbine school shooting changed it all. Before Columbine the protocol was to secure the perimeter and wait for SWAT. But that decision costs lives!

After Columbine, fire teams were developed and new methods of dealing with active shooters were implemented.

If an active shooter call comes in now, the first three or more officers form a fire team and seek to neutralize the shooter. You don't deal with the wounded or dying because that costs time, and lives.

You neutralize the shooter.

That may mean shooting him, or it may mean getting him into an area where he can't hurt anyone else.

Your priority is to **stop the killing!**

The father just happened to come home for a late lunch. He finds evidence that his 14-year-old son has come home from school for lunch for some reason.

There is a glass of milk and a half-eaten sandwich on the kitchen table. He decides to look around the house and find out why he's home from school.

The father goes into the basement he sees his gun cabinet is open. On the workbench is a sawed-off stock from his rifle. His mind reels in confusion. *Why?*

He sees a note in his son's handwriting saying, "They will pay."

The father does the right thing and he calls the police.

My partner and I arrive and start questioning the father.

"Where is he at, what school does he go to, what kind of weapon does he have, how much ammo is missing, what does your son look like?" I ask.

My partner and other officers head to the youth's school. I radio dispatch to put the school into lockdown. I stay and question the father.

I can hear the search on the radio of the school grounds, but they can't locate the kid.

Images of Columbine flowed through my head; *kids wounded and dying, others running from what is supposed to be a safe place.*

We have to find this kid before he hurts someone!

The father is crying, yelling in desperation, "Why?" as the enormity of the situation, shakes his entire body.

I'm thinking, *I have to find this kid, I need to ask the right question, I need to find him.*

A question enters my mind.

"How long has he been at this school?" I say

The sobbing parent says, "Only a month or so, he was kicked out of his previous school."

"Dispatch the youth is heading to his previous school, (I gave them the name) put it into to lockdown!" I yell into the radio.

My ears strain to hear the details on the radio as my fellow officers arrive at the new school.

"Units, he's on the hill near the front door, he spotted us, he's running into the coulee, he's got a rifle, I'm in a foot pursuit base," said the veteran K9 officer.

They chase the armed 14-year-old into a coulee, he turns towards the officers in pursuit, weapon in hand.

I can hear the commands over the radio, "DROP THE WEAPON, DROP THE WEAPON!"

I'm not even at the scene, and the adrenaline is rushing through me.

I look at the father thinking, *let him continue to be a father, don't let his son die!*

Through the radio I hear, "One in custody" and my whole-body sighs in relief.

"We have him, he's not hurt, and he hasn't hurt anyone," I say to the father. He collapses in relief.

Thoughts flood my mind: *So close, minutes from another disaster, one right question, one right answer."*

"WE'RE BACKING HIM, RIGHT?"

The "Peter Principle" is in full force in policing, the same way it is in other organizations. People rise to their level of incompetence.

A perfect example of this is a sergeant I have that was promoted, not for competence but for seniority.

This sergeant's style of policing is, to put it in a politically correct way, "antiquated".

His big thing is to stay in your zone. "If you're assigned to the north side, stay there no matter what."

This sergeant and I have had numerous, "run ins."

On one nightshift I am training a new rookie. We are assigned to the north side of the city. I requested and received permission from this sergeant that we can head to the south side for some follow-up.

Heading back to the north side after my follow-up, a fellow officer books out with three subjects in the parking lot of a golf course.

We're close, so I advise dispatch we're heading over. Immediately this sergeant gets on the air and says, "No, get back to your zone!"

Now, if it wasn't three in the morning and a fellow officer wasn't out with three subjects in a dark parking lot of a golf course, I might have headed back to my zone. But I can't risk this other officer's safety.

The rookie looks at me and says, "We're backing him, right?"

"Damn right!" is my reply, and we head to the golf course.

We arrive, but to prevent further problems with this sergeant I don't book out. We're just there to make sure the cop is safe.

Luck would have it, the bad guys had broken into the pro shop, and if we hadn't assisted the officer, the guys probably would have jumped him, and taken off. It was three to one.

We assist in the arrest of the bad guys, which lets the sergeant know we have disobeyed his orders.

When I get back to the station, the sergeant calls me into his office. He is mad. His face is red, and there was spit coming out of his mouth. He yells at me and threatens to charge me with disobeying his orders.

I reply, "If you think someone would convict me because I backed up a fellow officer, give it your best shot," and I walk away.

You must do what you believe is right. One of the main principles in policing is, "Have your fellow officer's back."

Always do, always will.

CONCLUSION: HOW IT ALL CAME TO BE....

I was born in Hamilton, Ontario, Canada. We moved around a lot through my childhood. My parents divorced when I was young, and I was raised primarily by Margaret Ward - my amazing, strong-willed, redheaded mother of eight.

I was always interested in the military. I successfully entered the Canadian Armed Forces Reserves in Toronto at age 15. I was good at high school football and baseball and was uncertain whether a career in sports or the military would unfold.

Often one significant event or action can change the course of your life. Sometimes it is obvious, sometimes not.

Driving home from the Armoury one night, dressed in my military uniform, my car started on fire. I pulled off Highway 427, and I quickly checked under the hood, found the engine in flames, and ran the half-mile to the Valhalla Inn for a fire extinguisher. When I returned to my car, I found the Fire Department putting out the flames. A young cop from the Toronto Police Service, 22 Division was also at the scene.

The young cop put me in the front seat of his Police Car, and we completed the necessary paperwork. He offered to drive me home to the East Mall. While on route to my home, a call came in about a break and enter underway at the West Mall. The cop noted my military uniform and decided I could ride along. Putting the pedal to the metal, we raced to the scene; my adrenaline was flowing freely! Arriving at the location, dispatch reported they had given the wrong address and redirected us to the East Mall shopping complex. The cop turned to me and asked, "You still want to come along?" to which I eagerly replied, "Hell, yeah!" We sped away with the lights and sirens blaring. When we got there, other officers had already arrived and taken charge of the scene, so the young cop drove me home. That event got me interested in policing. I knew that's what I wanted to do!

The next few years saw me move with my family to Kelowna, BC, Canada where I experienced other jobs and entrepreneurial endeavours. It is here I met my wife of 40 years. A construction career evolved, taking us to Calgary, AB and eventually back to the Okanagan Valley. Once again, I became involved with the Canadian Armed Forces in Kelowna, was commissioned as a Lieutenant, and fulfilled the role of a tank squadron commander. I hadn't the confidence to pursue a policing career until this time, but an opportunity arose with the RCMP Auxiliary Program. I applied and was accepted! My dream was coming true!

A series of doors proceeded to open and close in my life and ultimately led me to take a leap of faith that resulted in my successful entrance to the Law Enforcement Program at Lethbridge Community College, AB, Canada. I was hired to the police service a month before I even completed the program!

I often wonder what happened to that young Toronto police officer. His action of taking me along to a call inspired my rewarding, twenty-seven-year career in policing.

There is a quote that I put in the front of the notebooks I used in my policing career as a reminder to do what I can to help people. Whenever I took out my notebook I saw it. It is variant of an Edward Everette Hale's quote and reads:

I am only one,
But still I am one.
I cannot do everything,
But still I can do something;
And because I cannot do everything,
I will not refuse to do the something that I can do.

Do you care to make a difference in the world? Maybe an exciting career in policing is waiting for you too!

Randy Ward

Made in the USA
Lexington, KY
02 May 2018